Shaping Your Family's Future

Shaping Your Family's Future

Philhaven
Mt. Gretna, Pennsylvania

First published in 2007 by
Philhaven
283 South Butler Road, Mt. Gretna, PA 17064

ISBN-13: 978-0-9727077-4-9
ISBN-10: 0-9727077-4-3

Library of Congress Cataloging-in-Publication Data is available from
the Library of Congress.

Jacket design by Rule29
Interior design by Scribe, Inc.

First edition: June 2007

10 9 8 7 6 5 4 3 2 1

Printed in the United States of America.

Figure 14 is reproduced from David Olson, Douglas Sprenkle, and
Candyce Russell, "Circumplex Model of Marital and Family Systems:
Cohesion and Adaptability Dimensions, Family Types, and Clinical
Application," *Family Process* 18 (March 1979): 17, and used by permis-
sion from Blackwell Publishing, 9600 Garsington Road, Oxford, OX4
2ZG, United Kingdom.

Figure 15 is reproduced from Jack Balswick and Judy Balswick, *The
Family* (Grand Rapids, MI: Baker, 1999) and used by permission from
Baker Publishing Group.

Contents

List of Figures

Acknowledgments

Shaping Your Family's Future was born from a simple idea—that churches could do more to help families affirm positive attributes and break negative patterns passed from generation to generation.

Six years ago, Dale and Irene Weaver brought this vision to Philhaven, a church-related behavioral healthcare organization established in 1952 and located in South Central Pennsylvania. We shared this concern. Many persons could benefit from having the opportunity to consider what they have learned from their families of origin and to make choices about what they want to pass on to their children.

We needed to determine if this was a need that was felt by others. With the support of the United Service Foundation, a local family foundation of which the Weavers are a part, a feasibility study tested the need and vision with a wide variety of churches across the country. The consistent response was, "We would use this resource today if it were available."

The United Service Foundation generously agreed to fund the project and has provided helpful counsel throughout. A national advisory council was formed to help shape and guide the project. We are grateful to Kenton T. Derstine, Eastern Mennonite Seminary; Justin Lamason, Pastor of Family Life Ministries, Nappanee Missionary Church; Michael Schwartz,

Associate Pastor of Pastoral Care, North Anderson Church of God; Tony Gore, Counseling Minister, Southeast Christian Church; Linda Rump, Calvary Church, Roseville, Minnesota; Rev. Scott Ward, First Baptist Church, Dallas; Michelle Andres, Willow Creek Community Church; and Dr. Ron Hammer, Lake Avenue Church.

A local resource group provided additional input and helped to expand and strengthen the book's content. These persons included Janet Stauffer, Omar Zook, George May, Jim Johnson, Robert Reyes, and Dave Wolfe.

We must acknowledge the role of a few of the many other persons who helped make this resource possible. Mark Fretz (senior editor at Scribe, Inc.) offered expertise and connections in addition to managing the writing and publication processes, Marganne Hoffman's project management skills kept all of us on task, and Jim Shenk's counsel helped to negotiate the many decisions that needed to be made along the way.

Each person involved in this project has caught the vision of supporting parents in shaping their families' futures. We are grateful for their expertise, resourcefulness, and encouragement. It is our prayer that this book will be a helpful resource to parents, counselors, and congregations.

LaVern J. Yutzy
Chief Executive Officer
Philhaven
Mt. Gretna, PA
www.philhaven.org
May 1, 2007

Introduction

The Birth of a Family

How many hopes and fears, how many ardent wishes and anxious apprehensions, are twisted together in the threads that connect the parent with the child.

—Samuel Griswold Goodrich (Peter Parley)

Get ready for the wildest ride of your life! Being a parent can be the most thrilling, heartwrenching, and rewarding experience you'll ever have. But the truth is, parent*hood* is the easy part. To be a parent, all you need to do is to have a child. Parent*ing*, on the other hand, calls for real soul searching and a willingness to ask ourselves difficult questions. Parenting demands a clear understanding of what we're doing and why.

Make no mistake; parenting is not for the faint of heart. It takes more than a few trips to the baby store and a series of birthing classes to prepare for parenting. Over the next several weeks, *Shaping Your Family's Future* will introduce you to some important questions that you need to address. We'll help you develop the resources you need to parent with your eyes, mind, and heart wide open. The purpose of this book—and the related group sessions—is to help you understand the ways your family history shaped you and how that history affects you as a parent. In following this program, you will develop a perspective on parenting that allows you to make intentional choices about the kind of family life you want to have. Rather than blindly following the examples from your past, you can move into parenting confidently, knowing that you are making the choices you want to make for the good of your family.

In short order, you'll quickly discover that this is not your average parenting book. *Shaping Your Family's Future* does *not* equip you with practical parenting techniques. It won't tell you how to help your baby stop crying or fall asleep, or whether putting your baby to sleep on her back is better than on her side. It doesn't teach you how to make your child listen when she's throwing a tantrum. It doesn't give advice for a youngster's spiritual formation. In fact, we spend only a brief time actually discussing children. Instead, this book intends to guide you toward a deeper, more meaningful connection with your past and your future, so you can become the best parent you can be.

The six sessions of this course are demanding and intense, but, then again, so is being a parent. As you read *Shaping Your Family's Future*, you can think through and respond to the questions and discuss your thoughts and feelings with your spouse or with another person who may be committed to parenting with you. You can share insights with other group members and have your assumptions challenged. In doing so, you develop a clearer sense of how you view your self, your marriage, your family, the church, and the community around you. Your sense of who you are changes as you discover the importance of your role as a parent. Your relationship with your family and friends changes as you begin to see yourself as part of something far bigger than your own household. Your understanding of God also changes as you discover the ways in which parenting brings out a sense of life purpose you may never have experienced before.

Some of your ideas about parenting will change simply by reading this book. Families come in all sorts of shapes and sizes, and those aspects of your family can also change. The information and exercises in this book will be useful whether you are married or single, pregnant or adopting, creating a blended family or taking over the guardianship of a child, or already parenting a little one. Throughout, you will find the term *co-parent*. This might refer to your spouse, a friend, a neighbor, a grandparent, or anyone else who is committed to helping you shoulder parenting responsibilities; he or she will be a primary influence in the life of your child. You will find that as you expand your definition of "family," you'll begin to think about other people in your life differently. You may start to see your own parents, your child's caregiver at the daycare center or church, or a favorite neighbor as another partner in your parenting.

The concepts in *Shaping Your Family's Future* will also apply regardless of your own family background. You may have been raised in a home with two parents, a single parent, an older sibling or grandparent acting as your guardian, or as ward of the state in a group or foster home. You may have been part of a religious family or an agnostic family. You might have had a difficult childhood or a charmed, *Leave It to Beaver* kind of life. No matter what your personal history looks like, you will benefit from the concepts presented here.

Finally, *Shaping Your Family's Future* presumes that you parent your child in the context of other people, not in isolation. Parenting is never separate from the rest of your life or the people in your life. We know that families function as part of communities of faith, extended family, friends, and neighbors. Unlike most parenting books, this one pays special attention to you as a person, not just as a mother or father. *Shaping Your Family's Future* helps you look at your views on what it means to be a family. You think about what you believe is expected of you as a husband and father, or as a wife and mother. You discuss your views of discipline and how to handle conflict, church and community involvement, and the role of grandparents in your family life. Together with your co-parent, you talk about the kind of life you want to have with—and give to—your child.

Because parenting is rarely clear cut, each session offers many different points of view. There is time for group work and time to work one-on-one with your co-parent. A key feature of this book is that it points you toward the Bible for guidance. We show how faith plays a part in parenting. We also encourage you to share stories from your own family history. Your group facilitator will help you understand the basic material presented in *Shaping Your Family's Future*, but the flow of ideas in the group sessions is up to you. We hope that you become an active support network for one another as you venture into this new stage of life.

 Talk It Over

Think for a moment about what it means to you to be a parent. Then discuss the following with your co-parent:

- What part of parenthood are you most excited about? Or, if you already have a child, what *is* most exciting?

- What are you anxious about?

- What makes you nervous?

- In what ways do you think you will be a great parent? If you are a parent, identify one thing that you do that shows you are a great parent.

- Up to this point, where have you gotten most of your ideas about parenthood?

- Are there things you have vowed never to do as a parent?

- Is there any one thing you have promised that you will always do?

✠ Family Systems and Faith ✠

You don't have to dig very deeply into the Bible to see that the idea of the family system has been around since, well, the family. Scripture tells the story of God's family—warts and all—and the ways in which each generation chose to deal with the legacy left by the generation before it.

Some families function in a healthy way, others seem to self-destruct. There is certainly no shortage of dysfunction in the Bible's cast of thousands. Take a look at Jacob and Esau in Genesis 27, or the man who offers his daughter to a bunch of drunks in Judges 19:16–30. That's good to keep in mind as you dig into your own family issues. You may discover embarrassing, painful, even harmful parts of your family history. Remember, there is no such thing as a perfect family, and to expect perfection—that is, a family with no mistakes—is to set yourself up for disappointment. There is no shame in being part of a family that makes mistakes.

At the same time, remember that our parents and families possess valuable gifts and resources as well. In a literal sense, they made us who we are, with all the strengths, goodness, and potential to heal and make whole what is broken in our world. It is important to affirm about ourselves what God celebrated with the creation of the first man and woman: "Indeed, it was very good" (Genesis 1:31). So too, we should tap the blessings that our families offer us, embrace the wisdom they pass on to us, and lean on them when we need help.

Questions of faith and spirituality keep coming up throughout *Shaping Your Family's Future*. That's because we are, at our core, spiritual beings. That doesn't necessarily mean we all have the same understanding of God. It doesn't mean that we all live by the same set of religious expectations. Rather, it means that we all long for a sense of meaning in our lives. We want to believe our existence matters. We need to know that the world is somehow different because we are in it. These are spiritual longings. Questions of faith and spirituality are at the heart of who we are in the quiet of the night, when we are all alone.

These questions are the blueprints to what we want our lives to look like. So as you learn more about your views on faith, yourself, family, the church, and community, you'll find that none of these can be explored without the backdrop of spirituality.

The sessions are based on broadly held Christian beliefs. The ideas presented don't assume that everyone in the group comes from a single religious background. They don't point to one particular understanding of how to express your faith as a person or as a parent, because each person is unique. But the underlying idea throughout the book is that faith and spirituality are part of your family in some way and are therefore worth thinking and talking about when it comes to parenting.

The sessions also use the Bible as an authority for understanding our inner selves and our lives more clearly. The program is built on the belief that God's love for us is the source of all human love. And since healthy family life is, at its core, about loving one another, it's impossible to talk about parenting without the framework of God's love. After all, God's love created the first family: Adam and Eve. Genesis 2:18–24 tells us that God gave Eve to Adam as a gift of love, a way of making Adam's life complete. Together, they were given the role of caring for God's creation. Of course, that didn't go so well. Still, even in the face of their failure, God's love for Adam and Eve was unfailing. God told them to make a family, to pass the love they had been given on to their children. And so the story began. The family you are creating is a continuation of that same story, one that began with God's loving hands and that will carry on through your children and the generations to come. You're not simply adding a child to your family, you are adding a precious chapter to the story of God's work in the world. Exciting, isn't it?

Holding onto this broader perspective will help you let go of some of your anxieties about parenting. You aren't the first people to do this, nor will you be the last. You will make mistakes. But you'll never be without the guiding hand of God, who loves you and loves your children. God is big enough to redeem our greatest failures and build on our greatest successes as parents.

Along with this view of God's love we focus on God as being full of grace and mercy. Because we believe that God forgives us for all the ways in which we fail to be the people God created us to be, it's important that we learn to forgive others as well. Ephesians 4:31–32 says, "Get rid of all bitterness, rage and anger, brawling and slander, along with every form of malice. Be kind and compassionate to one another, forgiving each other, just as in Christ God forgave you." That is particularly applicable when it comes to family issues. It can be incredibly difficult to face the ways that our families have hurt us. Doing so means accepting our parents, and others we've been taught to respect, as flawed human beings who may have made terrible mistakes and hurtful choices. But learning to forgive and to extend grace to those who have hurt us is an essential step in becoming emotionally healthy adults. Forgiveness is no small thing, and it can be tempting to give it no more than lip service. But the beauty of exploring your family of origin is that you begin to see that even the most hurtful people in your past have redeeming qualities.

As you learn more about the childhood experiences of your parents and grandparents, you might find that they, too, have been hurt and damaged by those they trusted to care for them. They may have been scarred by the events of their lives in ways you've never thought about before. If you take nothing else from this course, try to find a place of compassion and mercy for those who have wronged you in some way. When you see the hurt child behind your father's rage or the bitter loss behind your sister's pettiness, suddenly your heart can open up and let go of the resentments and tensions that prevent you from extending grace and moving forward with a sense of peace and contentment. Our hope is that you learn how to love and forgive yourself, as well as your flesh and blood relatives.

✠ Your Other Family Tree ✠

You've probably realized that your role as a parent begins long before you ever hold a child in your arms. If you're pregnant, being a parent has already impacted the way you look and feel.

It alters your emotions and how you respond to people. It affects the way you eat and sleep. It changes the way you walk and breathe. Even if you're adopting a child, parenting has demanded your time and energy (the endless paperwork! the countless visits with the adoption agency!).

In truth, your notion of being a parent began back when you were just a child yourself. Becoming a healthy, confident parent involves understanding the things that shape us as people and as parents. One of the biggest factors that shape us as parents is the family in which we grew up—our *family of origin*. Naturally, genetics play a role in personality. Many of us grew up hearing messages such as "You've got your grandfather's sense of humor" or "You're stubborn like your mother." But these connections between you and previous generations run deeper than you think.

There's actually a fancy name for this perspective: Family Systems Theory (which we abbreviate as FST). FST is based on the idea that a person's family of origin influences the way a person thinks and feels about everything from marriage and intimacy to work and responsibilities. Certainly it colors the way a person acts as a parent. Someone brought up in a home with strict boundaries and firm discipline will have different ideas about parenting than someone who experienced few restrictions and little discipline. Whether you follow the pattern laid out by your family of origin or reject it completely, your actions and attitudes are still rooted in your family history.

The arrival of a new child means an addition to the family system. When one thing changes in a system, everything changes. Often a new mother will develop a rekindled closeness with either her own mother or other older female family members, establishing herself as a full-fledged member of their "adult" community. A new father might find himself feeling left out of the budding relationship between his wife and baby. Other relationships shift as well.

Take, for instance, Sarah. She and her older brother, Peter, were never close as kids, but when Sarah had children, Peter called more often and visited frequently. Suddenly, the brother Sarah had ignored for most of her adult life was in her living room several times a year. The more you understand about the ways that your family of origin operates, the better you can weather these shifts and use them to help you be a healthier person and better parent.

FST is a highly complex study of the emotional, psychological, and social connections that exist within families. Entire graduate courses are devoted to helping future therapists and counselors understand the various family-system models that have been developed over the years. *Shaping Your Family's Future* can only scratch the surface of all that FST entails. However, these sessions give you some basics to help you parent in a way that reflects where you have come from and where you want to go.

The basics of FST serve as the backbone for each session. Since these concepts can be a little complex and we didn't want to overload each chapter with too much theory, we provide a more detailed discussion of FST in Appendix A, at the back of this book. If you wish to find out more or to take a closer look at FST, feel free to return to Appendix A throughout the course; it also allows you to refresh your memory on what the concepts mean. For now, this brief description from the Bowen Center for the Study of the Family (http://www.thebowencenter.org) will be a good starting point:

> Bowen family systems theory is a theory of human behavior that views the family as an emotional unit and uses systems thinking to describe the complex interactions in the unit. . . . Family members so profoundly affect each other's thoughts, feelings, and actions that it often seems as if people are living under the same "emotional skin." People solicit each other's attention, approval, and support and react to each other's needs, expectations, and distress.

If you are married, you've undoubtedly bumped into the impact of your family system already (mother-in-law issues might come to mind). Mike and Kristin are a great example. Mike's parents both have quick tempers. They argue a lot, often in front of the kids. They tend to belittle each other and rarely come to any kind of resolution. Kristin's parents rarely argue. When they disagree, they prefer a kind of frosty silence. Eventually, they move on, not having openly discussed the problem. Like Mike's parents, Kristin's mom and dad rarely find any real resolution. So Mike and Kristin entered their marriage with very different expectations about conflict. The first time they argued about money Mike began to yell, and Kristin stormed out of the room and imposed a deep freeze on the relationship. You can imagine how well that worked. Mike and Kristin—like every couple—carried their families into their marriage, for better and for worse.

At the heart of FST is the idea of the family "rules" or expectations. Sometimes these are spoken, other times they are just silent assumptions—like the idea that conflict is bad. These rules aren't all negative. For example, Kyle's parents were both doctors, and both assumed that their children would take school seriously and work hard to do well in everything. There's nothing wrong with that. Other expectations can be more troubling. Jen grew up with a father who had a short temper. While no one ever said explicitly that the kids needed to work hard not to make Dad angry, the unspoken rule in her family was to stay out of Dad's way to avoid doing something that might incur his wrath. Much of your time over these six sessions is spent exploring the "rules" of your family of origin, as well as the way those rules impacted your beliefs about family and parenting.

Unless you enter parenthood with a clear awareness of the impact of these rules, you are likely to carry them into the family you are creating without even thinking about it. Once you've completed this course, you may find that you really like the rules you grew up with and want them to be part of your new family as well. If so, great!

One final note: As you dig into your family of origin, you may be surprised at what you uncover. You may find yourself laughing as you discover the key to a family quirk. You may find yourself thinking and talking about issues you haven't thought about in a long time. You may learn that your recollections don't match those of your parents or siblings. You may uncover difficult, even hurtful information about your family or your co-parent's family. If you begin struggling with issues that need to be handled in a more in-depth way, please talk with your group facilitator. He or she will be able to guide you to the kinds of resources—pastors, family counselors, support groups—that go beyond the help available in these group sessions. The *Shaping Your Family's Future* sessions are no substitute for professional marital or psychological counseling.

 Talk It Over

Talk with your co-parent about instances when you've run up against each other's family system. Be gentle here! Remember, it is not polite to climb around in your co-parent's family tree. You've got plenty of interesting characters and challenging relationships to deal with right at home. So, try to focus on seeing how your own family factors into your life, rather than pointing the finger at the quirks of your co-parent's family system.

- What are some ways your family of origin has helped your relationship?

- What are some ways it has created challenges?

- How have you dealt with these challenges?

Take a few minutes to think about your family of origin and some of the spoken—or unspoken—rules that governed how your family acted toward each other.

- What do you think are the three most important rules in your family of origin?

- How did you feel living under these rules and what were your reactions to them?

- Do you see yourself having similar expectations for your children?

Share your thoughts with the rest of the group and discuss how these rules might be shaping your expectations of parenting.

✠ Homework ✠

During the next six weeks, you'll be working on something called a *genogram*. Appendix B explains genograms in more detail, but for now, think of a genogram as a talking family tree. A typical family tree shows who was married to whom and who was born when, but a genogram also enables you to see patterns in family relationships. It helps put family relationships in perspective. Each session's homework assignment builds on the previous one, until at the end of the six sessions, you will have a complete and detailed genogram of your family.

The most valuable resources in finding out about your family are your mom, dad, brothers, sisters, grandparents, aunts, uncles, and cousins—that is, your family. For you to create your genogram, you will need to speak with family members, or at least try. As soon as you can, arrange one-on-one conversations with each of your siblings, your parents, and any living grandparents, aunts, and uncles. While the more people you talk to the more complete your family picture will be, don't worry if you can only make this happen with a handful of people. Face-to-face conversations may be more revealing, but phone calls, e-mails, and letters can be just as valuable. And don't get overwhelmed by the idea of having a series of long, intense discussions with people you may barely know. Start with one conversation and if it leads to more, that's great. Feel free to let Grandma or Auntie Sue just ramble a bit about their story, too. You never know what you'll discover!

Each chapter of *Shaping Your Family's Future* will wrap up with a homework assignment related to your genogram. In the instructions, you will find a list of questions that relate to that chapter's theme. These questions aren't meant to be a definitive list, but they should give you an idea of what is important—feel free to use as many or few as you like and to add your own. Really, the questions you ask are less important than the answers you get. As you talk to other members of your family, listen for the emotions behind the stories. Listen to what they *don't* say as well as what they *do* say. Look for patterns in relationships and recurrent themes, both within and across generations. Try to spot connections in family attitudes. The summary of FST in Appendix A offers some ideas on how to interpret the stories you hear.

This project can be incredibly helpful as you unpack your family history. Even if you know a lot about your family, the process of connecting the stories can reveal patterns you never noticed before. For example, as she did her genogram, Karen took a look at her relatives on her mother's side. She noticed that more than half of her mother's siblings had married alcoholics. In thinking over the stories she'd heard, Karen realized that her aunts and uncles often described their mother as a rather stoic woman. Many claimed she didn't do much in the way of emotional nurturing with her children. A few of them felt like they weren't wanted. Some said they felt like more of a bother than a source of joy. That may have led her children to seek out relationships where they felt needed and useful, a typical trait of codependent people—that is, people who are controlled by someone else, or function with a learned helplessness in relationships, often with others who have an addiction. This discovery helped Karen pay more attention to her own tendencies toward codependency.

The genogram you do for this program is a shorter version of a project that can take months, or even years. If you want to take a crack at a more detailed examination of your family, the book *Genograms: Assessment and Intervention*, by Monica McGoldrick, Randy Gerson, and Sylvia Shellenberger, is a terrific resource. You can find information on this and other resources at the end of this introduction and the end of each chapter.

Genogram—Step 1

For the first session, your homework is to create the basic framework of your genogram. See the more detailed description and samples of genograms provided in Appendix B for an explanation of how to start, what symbols to use, and what they mean. You can do this first step without even talking with family members, if you choose. However, it can be fun to get information or confirm what you know with you parents and grandparents.

Figure 1: Generic genogram

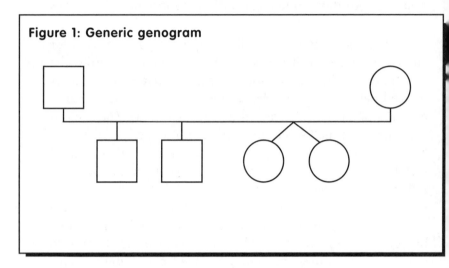

1. List the names of all the members of the immediate family in which you grew up (parents, siblings, those who lived in your home), all the members of the immediate family of each of your parents, and your grandparents' names. You should end up with three generations of your family.

2. For each person in these lists, gather as much personal information as you can. What is his or her full name? When was he or she born, and where? When was he or she married, and if applicable, when divorced? If someone died, when did that happen, and what was the cause of death?

3. Based on the information you gathered, organize family members by generation and in order of birth. Divide the page in half. At the top of the page, on the left half, draw a one-inch square for your dad's father (about an inch from the left margin), and a one-inch circle for his mother (about an inch to the left of center)—your paternal grandparents. Draw a short vertical line down from the square and circle, then connect the short vertical lines with a single solid horizontal line. This indicates that your father's parents were

married. If your grandparents are divorced, or in some other type of relationship, you should use a different type of symbol to connect the square and circle. For the correct symbol, look in Appendix B, under the explanation of genogram symbols, where it explains the interpersonal relationship symbols. Do the same on the right half of the chart for your mother's parents, with her dad's square about an inch right of the center line and her mom's circle about an inch left of the right margin. To the right of each square or circle, provide the person's name, and below the square or circle, list his or her birth date, including the full year (e.g., "b. 11/15/1909"). On the horizontal line, indicate the date they were married (e.g., "m. 5/10/1932"). If they got divorced, put two forward slashes next to each other in the middle of the line and indicate the date of divorce.

4. Add a short vertical line down from the horizontal "married" line between your father's parents for each of the children in your father's immediate family. Space these evenly on the line, listing the children in order of their birth, the oldest on the far left and the youngest on the far right. At the bottom of each of these vertical lines, draw a square or circle for a boy or girl, respectively. Next to each square and circle, list the name of the person, and below the square or circle, give the date of birth. Do the same for your mother's immediate family, on the right half of the genogram.

5. Draw a short vertical line down from your father's square on the left and your mother's circle on the right. Connect these two short vertical lines with a single solid horizontal line, as you did with your grandparents. On this horizontal line, indicate your parents' marriage date. If they are divorced, put two forward slashes next to each other in the center of the horizontal line and indicate the divorce date.

6. Repeat for your own immediate family what you did in Step 4 for each of your parents' immediate families. Add a short vertical line down from the horizontal line between your father and mother. List your siblings and yourself in birth

order, the oldest on the far left and the youngest on the far right. At the bottom of each of these vertical lines, draw a square or circle for a boy or girl, respectively. Next to each square and circle, list the name of the person, and below the square or circle, give his or her date of birth.

7. Draw a short vertical line down from your square or circle. Next to your symbol, draw a symbol for your co-parent and enter his or her name and birth date. Draw an appropriate connecting line between the two of you. If you are married, make it solid and indicate your marriage date. If you are in another type of relationship, indicate that using the appropriate symbol described in Appendix B. From the middle of this horizontal line (or marker), draw another short vertical line downward indicating your child, whether expected or already arrived.

After you finish this first step, your genogram should look something like the one on the following page.

 Talk It Over

As a group, talk about any thoughts you've had about what you've heard so far.

- Has the conversation raised any concerns for you?

- Has it given you something new to think about?

- Now that you know more about this class, what are you looking forward to?

Figure 8: Genogram Step 1: Basic family unit

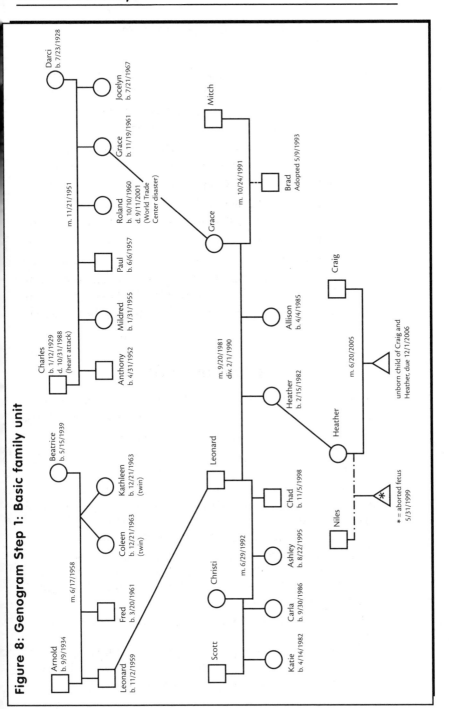

✚ Chapter Insights ✚

1. Although having a child makes you a parent, parenting requires that you work on many aspects of your inner self, your relationships with your co-parent and family, and perhaps most importantly your faith journey.
2. The family is a creation of God whose members, individually and collectively, benefit from cultivating a close and loving relationship with God. If in your role as a parent, you give the mercy and grace of God to others as freely as you have received it, you will shape your children's and family's future for the better.
3. Your family system influences the way you think and feel and how you will act as a parent. Each member of the family is connected to every other member in dynamic relationships, and each person's actions shape the family as a whole.

✚ Resources ✚

The Bowen Center for the Study of the Family (http://www.thebowencenter.org)
> A comprehensive site with a detailed description of Family Systems Theory.

Friedman, Edwin H. *Generation to Generation*. New York: Guilford, 1985.
> This academic book focuses primarily on family systems as they play out in religious communities, but there are valuable chapters on applying FST.

Foster, Carolyn. *The Family Pattern Workbook*. New York: Putnam, 1993.
> If you want to dig deeply into your family of origin and its impact on you, this guide can take you through a process of guided journaling.

Irving, John. *A Prayer for Owen Meany*. New York: Ballantine, 1990.
> A novel that beautifully illustrates the subtle influence of unspoken family rules, the impact of previous generations, and the power of the family story. If you prefer classics, try reading *Great Expectations* or *Wuthering Heights* for insights into family dynamics.

Kerr, Michael E., and Murray Bowen. *Family Evaluation*. New York: W. W. Norton, 1988.
> This book, intended for therapists looking for a way to help clients understand their families, is a useful—albeit heady—tool for parents who want to map out the impact of their family of origin in a more complete way.

McGoldrick, Monica, Randy Gerson, and Sylvia Shellenberger. *Genograms: Assessment and Intervention*. New York: W. W. Norton, 1999.

If you want to do a more in-depth genogram, this is the book to help you do it. The authors use the families of real historical figures to illustrate genogram principles. Not only will you learn more about your family, but you'll sound smart at parties, too.

Napier, Augustus Y., with Carl Whitaker. *The Family Crucible*. New York: Harper Paperbacks, 1988.

This narrative tells the story of a young girl who enters therapy with her family. This "see-it-in-action" approach can help readers develop a better understanding of how FST works.

Chapter 1

The Faith of Our Fathers (and Mothers)

The path of spiritual growth is a path of lifelong learning.

—M. Scott Peck

It may seem strange to spend time talking about faith formation in a parenting class. Yet your views of religion, the church, and spirituality are foundational to the kind of family you create. Every family, even those who don't really practice any kind of religion, holds some view of spirituality, the nature of God, and what it means to be a person of faith. A family might believe that faith is a crutch for the weak-minded. Or, they might believe faith is the rock upon which they build their lives (Deuteronomy 6:6–9). In either case, a family's view of spiritual issues enters every aspect of its collective experience. It informs the family's sense of purpose. It frames their philosophy about children. It impacts the way the family fits into its community. It influences how families spend their money, the activities in which the kids are involved, and how they celebrate holidays.

This session asks you to explore the messages of faith, spirituality, and God that you learned from your family of origin. As you get started, keep in mind that no two people have the same identical understanding of God, faith, religion, or spirituality. Even if several of the people in your group grew up in similar spiritual environments, or the same church, each of you will have a unique take on what that experience was like. You'll also have a different sense of how it affects you now.

✠ Spirituality and Humanity ✠

Spirituality is part of our humanity. We are created with an innate sense that there is more to life than just our physical existence. It's human nature to ask questions about our significance in the grand scheme of things, even if the answers we come up with say that there is no grand scheme of things. Our ideas and beliefs about spiritual issues flow into every aspect of our lives. They impact our work, our relationships, and our view of ourselves. Those elements of our lives in turn impact our spirituality. For example, a person who grows up in a home where the parents practice grace and compassion toward their children may be more inclined to see God as grace-filled and compassionate. A person who is constantly criticized at work or at home might start to question her value as a person and in turn question her value in the eyes of God.

That's why the first session in this course turns your attention to faith. In it, you begin to uncover some of the ways in which your family of origin shaped your spirituality. This chapter encourages you and your co-parent to discuss the messages about faith that you want to pass on to your children. You develop a deeper recognition of the role faith and spirituality play in other areas of your life. And that new understanding helps you get more out of the discussions of self, marriage, parenting, and community presented in the remaining chapters.

When you get right down to it, spirituality is essentially about relationships. It involves our relationship with a divine being, with creation, with other people, with ourselves. So it makes sense that we form our ideas about spirituality in the context of our primary human relationship: our family. It's within the family that we develop our sense of who we are and how we are to interact with the world around us. It's within the family that we figure out how to give and receive love. And it's within the family that we develop our view of authority and responsibility. Through our family we get a first glimpse of how God might act or think or value us. All of these factors work together to create our beliefs about God, faith, and religion.

It's impossible for one chapter to explain all the ways that your family of origin played a part in your spiritual life. Still, it can be helpful to start with a basic look at one of the core elements of spirituality that is deeply impacted by a person's family of origin: our view of God.

✛ Defining God ✛

At the heart of any understanding of spirituality and faith is a concept of a divine presence. Someone might define that presence as God or the Cosmos or a Higher Power, or someone might reject the concept altogether. In Genesis 1–2, the creation stories, God is a given; nothing would exist without divine action. No matter how you define this presence, it's part of the human experience to form some kind of belief about what or who is behind all of this. And your understanding of God is foundational to your sense of spirituality.

Obviously, the way we think about God is influenced by everything from our life experiences to the culture in which we are raised. Not surprisingly, a person's understanding of God is also deeply influenced by his or her family of origin. This influence comes through what family members say about the nature of God. It also comes through the subtle, even unconscious messages families send about God, God's relationship to the world, and the ways in which we relate to God.

At the same time, our view of God impacts the way we understand our relationships, our experiences, and ourselves. It impacts the decisions we make and the way we make them. It's no exaggeration to say that this view of God is at the core of who we are and how we live our lives. So it's worth taking the time to get to the heart of your ideas about God and the ways those beliefs influence you.

Certainly, a person's understanding of God is as unique and complex as that person himself. But for the most part, people tend to think of God in rather broad categories. In his book, *Your God is Too Small*, theologian J. B. Phillips detailed no less than thirteen different views of God that range from God as a warm, embracing source of comfort to God as a distant, uncaring source of disappointment.

In a moment, we'll look a bit more closely at a few of Phillips's conceptions of God. You might find that none of these completely match up with your view of God. Or you might find that there have been times in your life when you have had one or more of these views, depending on the circumstances. So don't get too hung up on the specifics of each view. Instead, think of this list as a starting point for a discussion about your view of God.

Resident Policeman

For many Christians, God's role in their lives is limited to their conscience. They equate God with that little voice in their heads that tells them what's right and what's wrong. This concept of God as a policeman might sound perfectly reasonable, especially if you are from a family that focused on proper behavior. It's based in the idea that faith is primarily about what we do, about living a good life. Based on the Old Testament law codes (Exodus 20–23; most of Leviticus; Deuteronomy 5–26) it is easy to understand when this concept of God originated.

Parental Hangover

The tendency to relate to God the way one relates to one's parents takes family-systems thinking to a slightly deeper level. While we have been discussing the ways your family of origin shaped your ideas about faith, Phillips notes that a person's family of origin—specifically a person's father—can often translate into that person's view of God. In other words, God can often look just like your father. If you had a positive, loving relationship with your father, that can be a very good thing. But if your relationship with your dad was filled with fear or fighting, or if it was abusive, well, that can lead to a serious faith crisis. Some parents can take the proverb, "spare the rod, spoil the child," too far (Proverbs 13:24).

> Sam grew up in a Christian family. His father was a harsh man who often literally beat his children into submission. Corporal punishment was his trusted method of discipline. He based his approach on what he perceived to be a biblical mandate for parents: use any means necessary to teach children to submit. When Sam or his brothers would misbehave, their father would read a passage of Scripture where God punished someone who had disobeyed God. He would then lash his child across the back of the legs with his belt. The message was that the child had not only failed his father, but failed God as well. Needless to say, Sam grew up with the belief that God was perpetually angry at him. As an adult, Sam battles bouts of depression and intense anger that are byproducts of his upbringing.

Given the countless examples of God punishing human sinfulness in the Bible—just read the books of Judges, Kings, and Chronicles—one can see why Sam's dad turned out the way he did.

Meek and Mild

Ironically, the view that God is meek and mild can be held by very faithful people as well as those who say they have no interest in spirituality. That's because in this view, God is a pushover. God is seen through the person of Jesus. And Jesus, in turn, is thought of as tender, gentle, and harmless—as the hymn by Charles Wesley goes, "Gentle Jesus, meek and mild." For many Christians, this perception of God is comforting. It makes God feel safe.

At the same time, this kind of God turns others away from religion. They don't want to put their trust in someone weak and easygoing. They want God to be a force, a rebel, or even a fiery righteous judge. Anything, they might think, except a wimp.

Managing Director

The idea that God is in his heaven directing life down here on earth is perhaps one of the most common views of God. Here again, some might find tremendous comfort in the belief that God is up there controlling all things and making the world turn each day. But for others, this kind of remote, big-picture type of God inspires little emotion or reaction. With God in a corner corporate office in the sky, they say, he can't relate to me. This view can also lead us to believe we are insignificant. Phillips points out that we think about our human ability to multitask and wonder how the God who is running things could possibly have time to notice each one of us individually.

 Talk It Over

Looking over the concepts of God presented here, talk about the way you see God.

- How did your family talk about God?

- Do any of the views discussed above describe your family's understanding of God? How are they different? How are they similar?

- What is your general sense of God?

- How do you think God is involved with humanity?

✠ Faith and Your Family ✠

Spiritual seeking and spiritual practices are reflections of our deepest self. That's why faith can be a flash point in relationships. For many people raised in religious families, rejecting the family religion can be a rite of passage. A person who sheds the family's shared beliefs often wants to show independence. An adult child who is more religious than his or her parents may have a difficult time relating to them. Over time this may create some emotional distance between parents and their adult children. Even subtle shifts away from the belief system of the family can create tension in the family dynamic.

When the next generation comes along—in the form of a new child—these differences often increase. New parents who are religious may not want their child to spend much time with grandparents who are not. If new parents approach religion more casually, the child's arrival might bring righteously charged pressure from more devout grandparents. Couples without children may deal with any religious differences that exist between them relatively easily. Once they become parents, however, and start making decisions about the faith they want to nurture in their child, tensions can easily bubble to the surface. What complicates conflicts over faith issues are the perceived high stakes involved—these are life and death decisions.

When Antawn was little, his parents took him to Saint Mary's Roman Catholic church. Janet, the young woman Antawn married in his mid-twenties, grew up attending the Maple Avenue AME church in town. When Antawn began dating Janet, neither of them saw their religious differences as an issue. On Sunday mornings, they went to their separate churches and reconnected afterward for brunch. But when they started talking about having children, they knew they would have to make a choice about their child's religious participation. During their conversations about this decision, both began to voice their beliefs about the shortcomings of the other person's faith tradition. Issues that they had easily ignored when it was just the two of them quickly emerged when they had to make choices for their child. The issues became even more exaggerated once their respective parents started weighing in with unsolicited advice.

In many families, religion acts as a line in the sand, where individuals can buy into the family's religious traditions, choose the exact opposite, or completely reject them lock, stock, and barrel. If we put these ideas in the terms of Family Systems Theory (FST), the first two responses to religion (buying in and choosing the opposite) are known as fusion. Emotionally, a family member who chooses to perpetuate the family pattern is engaging in positive fusion (where positive is not a value judgment, but simply describes one extreme of a polarity, like positive [+] and negative [-] battery terminals). Negative fusion amounts to choosing whatever is as different from the tradition as possible. Both options are fusion because the foundation of either choice is the same—the family tradition. The third response to religion FST calls cutoff. When someone chooses cutoff, he or she does away with the tradition altogether. Think of it as a merry-go-round: positive fusion is to push the ride clockwise, negative fusion is to push the ride counter-clockwise, and cutoff is to get off the ride and walk away, not caring which way the merry-go-round turns. Fusion keeps us connected emotionally one way or the other with the family, while through cutoff we make an emotional break from our family.

Our first ideas about faith are often borrowed from other people. Children typically have an understanding of faith that mirrors that of their parents. But as children grow up, they begin to formulate their own ideas about life and faith. Sometimes those ideas echo those of their family; other times they move to the opposite end of the faith spectrum.

Josh grew up in the Lutheran church. His father sang in the choir, and his mother was the Sunday School superintendent. While his family was very involved in the church, they were not a particularly "religious" family. Other than rote prayers at meals and bedtime, they didn't pray together much. They didn't have family devotions or read the Bible together. Josh never heard either of his parents talk about God or spiritual issues outside of church. Spirituality was essentially a Sunday morning routine. On occasion, Josh would hear his father make jokes about the "Bible thumpers" who lived next door, but that was the extent of the religious conversation in their home.

As he got older, Josh got involved in his church youth group because many of his friends were involved. He attended a private Lutheran college and eventually married his college girlfriend, Marie. He is now the father of two young children. They are members of a Lutheran church and attend Sunday services two to three times a month. Josh is an usher when needed and his wife helps out in the nursery. Like his parents, Josh is involved in the church, but participates in few private or personal spiritual practices apart from his Sunday morning duties.

Josh's wife, Marie, has started attending a women's Bible study at the church. Her involvement has inspired her to spend more time during the week reading her Bible and having short devotions with her children at bedtime. She would like Josh to be more involved in the children's faith formation, but Josh has resisted. He believes they will learn what they need to know in Sunday school. Josh has accused Marie of getting fanatical about religion. He is concerned she will turn their children into little "Bible thumpers."

Josh's story is an example of fusion, where he is repeating, rather than rejecting, what he learned from his parents. He has not thought through the questions of faith for himself. Josh has simply held onto his parents' view of spirituality and made it his own. This fusion to his family of origin becomes a problem when it gets in the way of Josh's relationship with his wife and children. If Josh wants to have a more real and fulfilling experience of faith, he may need to begin to recognize this fusion and make an effort to determine how he feels about spiritual issues for himself. The end results will be a more fulfilling relationship with his wife and a more fruitful involvement in the spiritual formation of his children, as well as cultivating his own spiritual growth.

Breaking the pattern of fusion doesn't mean Josh has to abandon what he learned from his parents. It's entirely possible for him to explore his ideas about spirituality and church and still end up in the same place as his parents. But in the process, he will have created genuine, interdependent points of connection with his family.

Ye Jin was raised in a conservative Korean Christian family. As a child, Ye Jin got the impression that God was a kind of benevolent ringmaster who made some things happen and prevented other things from happening. How and why God chose what to allow was beyond human comprehension. Until she was twenty-one, Ye Jin never questioned this understanding of God. But when her best friend was killed in a car accident, Ye Jin began asking why such a tragedy had to happen. Because of her family's faith messages, Ye Jin struggled to reconcile the conflicting idea of a loving God whom she could trust and God the ringmaster, who makes seemingly random decisions about who lives and who dies.

Over the next few years, Ye Jin's faith began to fade, and she became increasingly disinterested in church. By the time she was in her early thirties, she had no real desire for a relationship with God. Now Ye Jin is pregnant with her first child and has started thinking about her faith again. While she sees little need for church or God in her life, she has a hard time imagining her child growing up without some kind of religious experience.

Ye Jin's distance from her church roots has been difficult for her parents. She sees their prompting as nagging, and religion has become a point of tension in their relationship. As a result, for several years Ye Jin has avoided contact with her parents whenever she could. She rarely visits or calls home. When she does, she consciously steers the conversation away from religion. Ye Jin's parents have taken her hints and, in an effort to maintain some connection with their daughter, have stopped talking with her about her faith. But now that their first grandchild is on the way, they are increasingly concerned. They worry that this child will be raised outside of the church. However, they don't dare bring up the issue with Ye Jin for fear that they will be cut off from her and her child.

For Ye Jin, religion has become a point of emotional cutoff with her family of origin. By keeping the subject off-limits, Ye Jin has put up a barrier that will prevent her from having a healthy connection with her parents. Like Josh, Ye Jin has carried her childhood messages about faith into adulthood without really examining them. While the end result has been different, both Josh and Ye Jin have let their family of origin dictate their spiritual lives.

Talk It Over

- Can you recall the three most vivid memories from your childhood of your family's religious practice?

- What are some areas where you remain fused to the faith expressions of your family of origin or rejected them?

- What assumptions do you make about God, the church, and religion that you can trace to specific messages from your family of origin?

- What messages about faith do you find helpful in your spiritual journey? What messages are unhelpful?

- What spiritual messages do you want to pass on to your children? How do you see yourself doing that?

- What spiritual practices do you want to make part of your family life?

✠ Changing Faith ✠

Many new parents are surprised to discover that the arrival of a child leads them to think about their faith in new ways. The new responsibilities of parenthood often make us more aware of our mortality and our vulnerability. This can lead some parents into a kind of faith crisis, while others will find their faith growing stronger.

Sarah found that when her first child was born, she had a hard time trusting God. She was surprised by how much she feared something bad happening to her baby. She shared these fears with her husband who told her, "Honey, you know God will take good care of our baby." When Sarah heard this, her first thought was, "No, he won't." Sarah had of God as "the Judge who will punish wrongdoing." Sarah had never really questioned that inherited image of God before she became a mother. While she kept telling herself she was being ridiculous, Sarah couldn't shake the fear that God might let her baby die to punish Sarah for her sins.

When Amanda became a mother, on the other hand, she felt her faith becoming deeper. Like Sarah, Amanda grew up in a religious family. But her image of God was as a comforting, loving Father. When Amanda and her husband adopted a little boy, she began to understand God's love for her in a new way. She says, "Now I know what it means to love someone so much you can forgive them no matter what they do, to love them so much you would give your life to save theirs." Amanda also experienced the fear of something bad happening to her baby. But she was able to find comfort in her understanding of God as her protector. Her sense of vulnerability was quelled by her belief that God would meet her needs as a mother and help her care for her son.

The ways in which your faith will shift when you become a parent are obviously impossible to predict. You can, however, get some hints by looking at your family of origin. Spirituality and messages about faith often play out in subtle ways. You might not be able to put your finger on any specific messages right away. But, with a little thinking, you should start to discover the connections between your spiritual life and that of your family of origin.

Every family creates a legacy of faith. Sometimes that legacy is laced with beautiful expressions of authentic, life-sustaining faith. Other times, it's a heritage of hurt and manipulation. Whether your story has brought you to a place of peace or conflict, joy or pain, it's your story and it matters. As you move through the remaining chapters of *Shaping Your Family's Future*, you will revisit the ideas you have dealt with in this chapter, for they are central to the person you are today and the family you are inaugurating in the near future.

✠ Homework ✠

This week, you set off on a voyage to explore your family of origin using the genograms as your vehicle. You'll use your genogram project to explore the views of spirituality, faith, God, church, and religion that are part of your family heritage. Talk with your family members individually—mom, dad, brothers, and sisters first, then the extended family as time and energy permits—about these issues, but keep in mind that faith can be a very difficult thing for some people to talk about. Still, even the fact that it's hard to talk about can be a hint about your family's view of faith.

Genogram—Step 2

1. Write down your own recollections of religious practices that your family kept. The focus is on the family as a unit, rather than on you as an individual within the family.

2. Write down your memories of meaningful religious and spiritual experiences or insights. The focus here is on your own personal spiritual and religious journey.

3. Describe in a list of bullet points the beliefs and values that form the core of your family's religious tradition. This list differs from practices in that beliefs and values serve as the underlying principles that provide the reason for the religious tradition.

4. Talk with your family members about their views, memories, beliefs, and practices. Look for any "Aha!" moments, surprises, or recurring themes in the things you hear. What do these conversations tell you about your own faith formation?

Your genogram begins with you and your faith experience. From there you can add other individuals and your connections with them. But in Chapter 2, we focus on the place you occupy within the triangles of your family system. Here are some questions to get you started:

- In your growing-up years, how often did your family attend some kind of religious event (including worship services, community events of a religious nature, rallies or crusades, house church meetings, prayer meetings, Bible studies, etc.)?
- Who was expected to attend these events?
- What was your sense of how your parents felt about these events?
- What kind of religious events did you participate in as a child (Sunday school, Vacation Bible school, weeknight activities, release time from public school for religious education, summer church, Bible camp, etc.)?
- What routine spiritual practices were important in your family (prayer, personal devotions, meditation, etc.)?
- Did your family talk about religion, and if so, where, when, and how? Around the dinner table? In the car on the way to church? At large family gatherings?
- In what ways did the messages about religion change when there were other people—grandparents, neighbors, business associates—around?
- Did religion ever stir up conflict in your family?
- Once you became an adult, what expectations did your family have for your faith and spiritual life?
- How would you sum up your family's understanding of spirituality and faith?

5. Once you gather all the information you can about your family's religious traditions, enter on the genogram indications of each individual's religious affiliation, as well as the family's religious traditions. To the left of each square or circle, add the symbol and number indicating that person's

Figure 9: Genogram Step 2: Faith traditions of the family

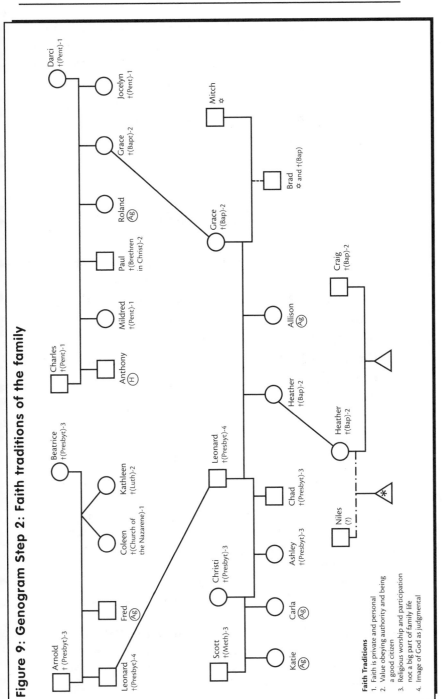

Faith Traditions
1. Faith is private and personal
2. Value obeying authority and being a good citizen
3. Religious worship and participation not a big part of family life
4. Image of God as judgmental

religious affiliation and level of commitment. For example, if your mother was a devout Roman Catholic, next to her circle put a cross symbol and the word Catholic in parentheses, followed by a hyphen and 1: ✝(Catholic)-1.

6. On the lower left-hand corner of the genogram, write "Religious Traditions" and enter key words that indicate the religious beliefs and values that form the core of the family's religious traditions.

✚ Chapter Insights ✚

1. You are a spiritual being, in your role as parent, spouse, child, sibling, coworker, or in the solitude of your life.

2. Your family shapes your understanding, experience, and expectations of God, as do your faith community and your own musings about the divine realm.

3. Children inevitably force parents to think about and try to explain their faith in ways that help the child begin to form his or her spirituality.

✚ Resources ✚

Jones, Tony. *The Sacred Way: Spiritual Practices for Everyday Life*. Grand Rapids, MI: Zondervan, 2005.

A helpful, practical resource for those looking to introduce intentional spiritual disciplines like silence and solitude, prayer, and meditation into their lives.

Peace, Richard. *Spiritual Autobiography: Discovering and Sharing Your Spiritual Story*. Colorado Springs: NavPress, 1998.

Creating a spiritual autobiography can be a wonderful way to trace the formation of your faith. This guide provides questions and ideas to spark your thinking.

Phillips, J. B. *Your God is Too Small*. New York: Touchstone, 1997.

A quick little book that packs a wallop. Phillips outlines several ways people think about God and challenges readers to make way for a bigger, more expansive understanding of the Creator of the world.

Potok, Chaim. *The Chosen*. New York: Fawcett, 1987.

———. *My Name is Asher Lev*. New York: Anchor, 2003. Both of these classic novels deal with the struggles of young boys who bear the heavy weight of carrying on the family faith tradition. Beautifully written and deeply moving.

Walsh, Froma. *Spiritual Resources in Family Therapy*. New York: Guilford, 2003. Walsh and other therapists created this resource to help therapists work with their patients' spiritual issues. While it can be a bit technical, it's also very insightful for those who need to recover a healthy understanding of spirituality.

Chapter 2

Getting to Know You

*What we think we have discovered about ourselves is very
superficial at first, so that real self-knowledge only
comes after years of patient effort.*

—Harry Benjamin

There's an old saying that the only constant in life is change.
That is perhaps most true when it comes to who you are
and who you are becoming. As children we tend to think of
adults as complete or finished. Our belief is that adulthood is
the final stage of development. Once we get to be adults, we'll
be done with the mess of trying to figure ourselves out. But
when we become adults, we realize that nothing could be further from the truth.

In many ways, our sense of ourselves changes more during
adulthood than at any other stage of life. These are the years
when we are all too aware of our flaws and failures. This is the
time of life when we put ourselves out there to get a job or find
a mate, only to be reminded of all the ways we don't measure
up. Unfortunately, the situation doesn't necessarily improve
when we become parents. In fact, this is one of the greatest

ironies of parenting: The role you thought might finally make you feel like an adult more often than not makes you realize how much you still have to learn. But that's what makes this the perfect time to take a closer look at how you view yourself.

Think of this process as "unpacking" your family baggage, where you take out the pieces of your identity and decide which ones can still hang in your closet and which ones you ought to toss in the give-away pile. Doing this requires two things: First, you need an objective assessment of messages you received about yourself from your family. Second, you need to understand your subjective view of the way you see yourself functioning in the world. Once you have a stronger grasp of the ways your self-concept has been shaped, you'll understand yourself better and have the tools you need to be intentional about shaping your child's sense of self. In short, you'll be better equipped to make parenting decisions. Your choices will be based on who you really are and what you really value, rather than on the roles and values you *think* you should have.

✚ The Family Dance ✚

The way a person's identity is formed is as unique as the person herself. Your biological make-up mixes with your family environment, your culture, and your unique experiences to make you you. That lively jumble of ingredients makes it difficult to discuss personality and self-concept in any concrete way that applies to everyone. What is true for one person is rarely true for everyone else. This session, then, is not meant to tell you who you are. It is meant to help you think about the way you see yourself.

Most people's self-concept is bound up in the fabric of their families of origin. Therapists often call the ways individuals within a family system relate to one another the "family dance." So, get the image of a ballroom dance in your head for a minute. In ballroom dancing, a dancer has an intuitive sense of how his or her partner moves and how to respond to those movements.

Each partner has a feel for how to keep the dance flowing. In a family, each member learns to move and respond to the other members in particular ways intended to keep the family system working. A move by one person requires the rest of the family to react and adjust.

Maybe you had a strong mother in your family, who led the dance by setting the expectations for behavior. Everyone else then learned to respond to her in one way or another. Or it might be that you had a troubled sibling who became the lead dancer by moving the family in a certain direction, and everyone else followed along. You may think of your family as a fluid waltz, as a jumbled mess of stumbling movement with countless toes stepped on, or as a mix of both. Regardless of the kind of dance your family has, seeing your own steps in that dance is part of understanding yourself.

Aretha is the older of two children. When Aretha was ten, her younger sister Mandisa died of leukemia. The loss of their daughter was obviously devastating to Aretha's parents. Aretha watched her parents grieve and knew that she never wanted to be the cause of additional suffering in their lives. So Aretha worked hard in school, volunteered in her community, and was careful to avoid upsetting her parents in any way. For their part, in the years following Mandisa's death, Aretha's parents doted on her, taking her on skiing vacations and trips to Disney World, buying her a car when she turned sixteen, and paying for a lavish wedding when Aretha married her husband Malcolm.

But once Aretha was married, she began to get annoyed at her parents' neediness. They often invited Aretha and Malcolm to go on vacation with them. Her parents even offered to pay their way to make it easier for them to come along. Even though Aretha and Malcolm lived an hour away from her parents, Aretha's mother called at least once a week to see if she and Aretha could meet for lunch. When Aretha and Malcolm decided to spend Christmas with his family out of state, Aretha's parents arranged to stay in a hotel in the same town so that they could spend part of the holiday with their only child. Malcolm encouraged Aretha to let her parents know that they needed to give her and him a bit more space. Aretha resisted; she didn't want to upset them. Even though she was irritated at her parents and felt smothered by their constant attention, Malcolm's suggestion made her uneasy because she knew they were just trying to stay connected to their only child. Aretha didn't want to hurt them, so she kept her feelings to herself.

In Aretha's family, the dance steps went like this: The death of Aretha's sister set the stage. Even though she was dead, Mandisa was the lead dancer. Her death led the family from that point on. In response, Aretha's parents changed their dance steps so that they seemingly revolved around Aretha. They had in fact kept dancing with Aretha's sister in response to their grief. Aretha responded to her sister's death by becoming compliant. She did her best never to cause her parents more pain than what they had already experienced. As an adult, Aretha continued the dance by accepting her parents' excessive attention and complying despite her discomfort.

Even when the family dance is awkward or uncomfortable, it can be difficult to break the pattern. That's because everyone involved in the dance has an interest in seeing it continue. We are comfortable with our role in the dance because it's predictable, not necessarily because we like our role. We know what is expected. It simply becomes second nature to fulfill our role. To break out of the dance means risking the security and comfort that come with playing our assigned parts. In Aretha's case, she resisted confronting her parents' excessive attention because she was afraid of the fallout. Her fear of making a change in the dance outweighed her discomfort with their tendency to be overly involved in her life.

In some cases, the family dance doesn't center on a person, but on an event or situation. The lead dancer may be a family member's addiction, a historical event, or some kind of abuse. In these families, members assume roles related to this lead issue. Often these family dances involve secrecy, blame, and shame. Ironically, the individual exhibiting unhealthy behavior or demanding attention may unconsciously be attempting to turn up the emotional heat so that the family as a whole will be forced to change the way it dances. If, for example, a "troubled" teenager suddenly becomes a suicidal teenager, the family dance shifts. Where the teen may have once been the instigator, she is now seen as the victim or the patient, which causes everyone else to regroup and find new roles as well. (One note: If your family dance includes some kind of abuse—sexual, physical, emotional, or spiritual—or addiction, please seek professional counseling, if you haven't already. It's essential to your health as a human being, and your success as a parent, that you rescue your true self from the pain of your past. This may be the only way to prevent yourself from passing on your emotional pain to your children.)

That said, the family dance is not necessarily a negative phenomenon, either entirely or in part. There are plenty of families in which the dance is both functional and mutually satisfying to everyone involved. Many people find tremendous strength in knowing that they have a crucial place in a family system. A healthy family dance creates the sense of belonging we all long for in our families. This sense of connection is one of the many gifts God gives us through the family unit. In the family of Jesus' friend Lazarus, sisters Mary and Martha each played a unique part (Luke 10:38–42).

The purpose in taking a closer look at your family's dance is not to cut in suddenly and make everyone change their steps. Rather, the purpose of bringing the family dance into the light is to notice the ways in which the dance has shaped your understanding of yourself and your place in the world.

This process is empowering because it reminds us that we don't have to be caged in by this dance. Each member of the family can change his or her role over time. Recognizing this frees you from assuming that each person always has performed—and must continue to perform—the same steps in the family dance. It empowers you to choose which steps you want to participate in. It gives you the option to break habits or patterns of behavior you may have embraced in the past. It also reminds you that other members of your family have permission to change and grow, too. Ultimately, you need to be willing to let them change their steps along with yours.

Looking at Aretha's story, we can see why she feels deeply loved by her parents. Their attention and affection clearly created closeness between the three of them that has lasted into Aretha's adulthood. So Aretha's role in her family dance had a number of positive effects on her sense of herself. She knows she is valuable, lovable, and worthy of her parents' time and attention. Because she watched the intensity of their grief, she has a profound understanding of the love her parents have for their children. Aretha has never questioned her self-worth or longed for her parents' affection.

At the same time, Aretha sees herself as the source of her parents' strength. Even as a teenager, Aretha took great pains to put on a happy face for her parents and rarely complained about anything. In fact, she tried to make sure they were never disappointed with her. This largely self-inflicted pressure to perform has caused Aretha to wrestle with perfectionism. As is true of any marriage, Aretha and Malcolm often disagree and argue about the basics of sharing a life—finances, the division of housework, and sex. But because Aretha always worked so hard not to rock the boat at home, it's hard for her to deal with these conflicts in her marriage. For Aretha, love had always been defined by the lack of conflict or dissatisfaction, so she winds up wondering if her husband really loves her. Aretha tries to smooth over any conflict in the relationship, often ignoring her own needs and simply agreeing with her husband's point of view. In place of asserting herself, she simply promises herself she will try harder to do better at meeting his needs and keeping him happy.

The dance carried on by Aretha's family of origin clearly played a part in forming her self-concept. The same is true for each one of us. Our intimate relationships—particularly those between family members—are complex and constantly evolving. Making the connections between our family systems and our understanding of ourselves takes intentional effort and effective tools. One such tool is the Enneagram—an assessment of the combination of characteristics that make up your relational pattern.

Talk It Over

While Aretha's story points to a clear beginning of the family dance (the death of her sister), other family dances may have more subtle beginnings. The family dance can revolve around a family member with special needs or someone with addiction issues. The lead dancer can be someone with a short temper or someone who stands out as gifted or "special." This person may have no conscious intention of setting the tempo for the family, or they may be very aware of how they manipulate others. As you think about your family's dance, consider these questions:

- Who is the lead dancer in your family of origin? How did that person get that role?

- How did that person set the pace for the rest of the family?

- What are the unspoken expectations in your family's dance, of each individual and of the family as a unit?

- What roles did your family members play in this dance? Who are the leaders? The followers?

- Would the other members of your family answer these questions about roles and who was the leader differently?

- Did anyone in your family ever try to change the dance by no longer acting as was expected? What happened?

✠ The Enneagram ✠

The goal of this journey of self-discovery is not to descibe your-self in fifty words or less. It is to recognize the way you tend to think and feel, the desires and needs that typically drive you. Being an introvert or extrovert in itself is neither good nor bad. However, knowing that you are clearly one of the two should help you respond to an invitation to give a speech in front of five hundred people. Once you have a grasp of who you are, you can be more purposeful about tending to those parts of yourself that are helping you become the person you want to be. You can also become more effective at weeding out those parts that are getting in your way.

There are all kinds of resources to help you develop a bet-ter understanding of your relational pattern. Some of these are more helpful than others. The Enneagram (pronounced 'en-nee-a-"gram, from the Greek words *ennea* [nine] and *gramma* [something written or drawn]) can be helpful in iden-tifying relational patterns.

The Enneagram is a set of nine relational patterns. These patterns are very broad, but they give helpful insights into the way we view the world, make decisions, react to people, and deal with stress. Most importantly, they help identify the desires and fears that drive us to think and act in particular ways. Don Riso and Russ Hudson, the developers of the Enneagram Type Indicator, identify the nine relational patterns of the Enneagram by both a number and a name. While the names are helpful labels, they can also feel a bit limiting. For example, if you discover you are an Eight—the Challenger—that doesn't mean you are always assertive. Nor does it mean you are not also loyal or helpful or enthusiastic. So as you read through the following descriptions, don't get hung up on the labels. Instead, look over the descriptions and choose two or three that sound like you. Keep in mind that the descriptions presented here only provide an overview and not the full picture of each relational pattern. The relational patterns (as explained in Riso and Hudson 1999, 11–12) are:

Reformer
Helper
Achiever
Individualist
Investigator
Loyalist
Enthusiast
Challenger
Peacemaker

Relational Pattern One: The Reformer

The Reformer exhibits a principled, idealistic relational pattern. Ones are ethical and conscientious, with a strong sense of right and wrong. They are teachers and crusaders, like John the Baptist and the prophets of Israel. They always strive to improve things, but are afraid of making mistakes. Well-organized, orderly, and fastidious, they try to maintain high standards, but can slip into being critical and perfectionistic. They typically have problems with repressed anger and impatience. *At their best*, healthy Reformers are wise, discerning, realistic, and noble, as well as morally heroic.

Relational Pattern Two: The Helper

The Helper exhibits a caring, interpersonal relational pattern. Twos are empathetic, sincere, and warm-hearted. They are friendly, generous, and self-sacrificing. They can also be sentimental, flattering, and people-pleasing. They are driven to be close to others, and they often do things for others in order to be needed, such as John the beloved disciple of Jesus. They typically have problems taking care of themselves and acknowledging their own needs. *At their best*, healthy Helpers are unselfish and altruistic and have unconditional love for themselves and others.

Relational Pattern Three: The Achiever

The Achiever exhibits an adaptable, success-oriented relational pattern. Typically, Threes are self-assured, attractive, and charming. They are ambitious, competent, and energetic. Think of King Solomon. They can also be status-conscious and highly driven for personal advancement. Threes are often concerened about their image and what others think of them. They typically have problems with workaholism and competitiveness. *At their best*, healthy Achievers are self-accepting, authentic, and everything they seem to be—role models who inspire others.

Relational Pattern Four: The Individualist

The Individualist exhibits a romantic, introspective relational pattern. Fours are self-aware, sensitive, reserved, and quiet. They are self-revealing, emotionally honest, and personal. They can also be moody and self-conscious. They can withhold themselves from others due to feeling vulnerable and defective. Fours can also feel disdainful and exempt from ordinary ways of living. They typically have problems with self-indulgence and self-pity. *At their best*, healthy Individualists are inspired and highly creative, able to renew themselves and transform their experiences.

Relational Pattern Five: The Investigator

The Investigator exhibits an intense, cerebral relational pattern. Fives are alert, insightful, and curious. They are able to concentrate and focus on developing complex ideas and skills. Independent and innovative, they can become preoccupied with their thoughts and imaginary constructs. They become detached, yet high-strung and intense. They typically have problems with isolation, their behavior may appear weird to others, and they can seem to act as if nothing matters except what serves their interests—as if they are living in their own world. *At their best*, healthy Investigators are visionary pioneers.

They are often ahead of their time and able to see the world in a new way.

Relational Pattern Six: The Loyalist

The Loyalist exhibits a committed, security-oriented relational pattern. Sixes are reliable, hardworking, and responsible. They can also be defensive, evasive, and highly anxious—running on stress while complaining about it. They are often cautious and indecisive but can also be reactive, defiant, and rebellious. They typically have problems with self-doubt and suspicion. *At their best*, healthy Loyalists are internally stable, self-confident, and self-reliant. They courageously support the weak and powerless.

Relational Pattern Seven: The Enthusiast

The Enthusiast exhibits a busy, productive relational pattern. Sevens are versatile, optimistic, and spontaneous. They are playful, high-spirited, and practical. They can also be overextended, scattered, and undisciplined. They constantly seek new and exciting experiences, but they can become distracted and exhausted by staying on the go. They typically have problems with superficiality and impulsiveness. *At their best*, healthy Enthusiasts focus their talents on worthwhile goals, becoming joyous, highly accomplished, and full of gratitude.

Relational Pattern Eight: The Challenger

The Challenger exhibits a powerful, dominating relational pattern. Eights are self-confident, strong, and assertive. They are protective, resourceful, and decisive. They can also be proud and domineering. Eights feel that they must control their environment, often becoming confrontational and intimidating. They typically have problems allowing themselves to be close to others. *At their best*, healthy Challengers are self-mastering—they use their strength to improve others' lives, becoming heroic, magnanimous, and sometimes historically great.

Relational Pattern Nine: The Peacemaker

The Peacemaker exhibits an easy going, self-effacing relational pattern. Nines are accepting, trusting, and stable. They are good-natured, kindhearted, easygoing, and supportive. They can also be too willing to go along with others to keep the peace. They want everything to be without conflict but can tend to be complacent and minimize anything upsetting. They typically have problems with passivity and stubbornness. *At their best*, healthy Peacemakers are indomitable and all-embracing. They are able to bring people together and heal conflicts.

Identifying Your Relational Pattern

Now, look over the two groups of paragraphs that follow. In each group, choose *one* paragraph that most closely describes your general behavior and attitude over the course of your life. Keep in mind that you probably won't agree with every word in a given paragraph, so choose the one that seems most like you. Don't overanalyze, just trust your instincts on this and go with the one that fits you best. When you're done, you should have a pair of letters—one from Group 1 and one from Group 2.

Group 1:

A. I have tended to be fairly independent and assertive. I've felt that life works best when I meet it head-on. I set my own goals, get involved, and want to make things happen. I don't like sitting around—I want to achieve something big and have an impact. I don't necessarily seek confrontations, but I don't let people push me around, either. Most of the time I know what I want and go for it. I tend to work hard and play hard.

B. I have tended to be quiet and am used to being on my own. I usually don't like to draw much attention to myself socially, and I tend not to assert myself all that forcefully. I don't feel comfortable taking the lead in competitive situations, as much as others do. Many would probably say that

I'm something of a dreamer—a lot of my excitement goes on in my imagination. I can be quite content without feeling I have to be active all the time.

C. I have tended to be extremely responsible and dedicated. I feel terrible if I don't keep my commitments and do what's expected of me. I want people to know that I'm there for them and that I'll do what I believe is best for them. I've often made great personal sacrifices for the sake of others, whether they know it or not. I often don't take adequate care of myself—I do the work that needs to be done and relax (and do what I really want) if there's time left over.

Group 2:

X. I am the person who usually maintains a positive outlook and feels that things will work out for the best. I can usually find something to be enthusiastic about and different ways to occupy myself. I like being around people and helping others to be happy—I enjoy sharing my own well-being with them. (I don't always feel great, but I try not to show it to anyone). However, staying positive has sometimes meant that I've put off dealing with my own problems for too long.

Y. I am a person who has strong feelings about things—most people can tell when I'm unhappy about something. I can be guarded with people, but I'm more sensitive than I let on. I want to know where I stand with others and who and what I can count on—it's pretty clear to most people where they stand with me. When I'm upset about something, I want others to respond and to get as worked up as I am. I know the rules, but I don't want people telling me what to do. I want to decide for myself.

Z. I tend to be self-controlled and logical—I am uncomfortable dealing with feelings. I am efficient—even a perfectionist—and prefer working on my own. When there are problems or personal conflicts, I try not to bring my feelings into the situation. Some say I'm too cool and detached, but I don't want my emotional reactions to distract me from what's really important to me. I usually don't show my reactions when others "get to me."

Once you have selected the two paragraphs that best describe you, use this chart to determine your relational pattern:

Combination	Relational Pattern
AX	Seven: The Enthusiast
AY	Eight: The Challenger
AZ	Three: The Achiever
BX	Nine: The Peacemaker
BY	Four: The Individualist
BZ	Five: The Investigator
CX	Two: The Helper
CY	Six: The Loyalist
CZ	One: The Reformer

One aspect of the Enneagram that makes it different from other kinds of personality tests is that it is actually not about personality at all. The creators of the test are quick to point out that the Enneagram is meant to help us move past our personalities and discover the fundamental essence of who we are. It is designed to help discern the ways in which we are each a unique reflection of the image of God.

The Bible gives us plentiful examples of God embodying each of the nine relational patterns:

Relational Pattern	Examples
God as Reformer	Isaiah 52:9; Revelation 21:5 (and really, the entire story of God's redemptive work in the world)
God as Helper	Genesis 49:25; Exodus 18:4; Psalms 10:14; 40:17; 46:1
God as Achiever	Exodus 23:19; Isaiah 48:17; Philippians 1:6; 4:8
God as Individualist	Deuteronomy 4:35; 1 Kings 8:60; Isaiah 44:8
God as Investigator	1 Samuel 2:3; Job 28:20–24; Psalms 139:23

Relational Pattern	Examples *(continued)*
God as Loyalist	Genesis 6:18; 15:18; 24:27; Deuteronomy 4:31; Nehemiah 9:31; Romans 15:8
God as Enthusiast	Psalms 19:8; Isaiah 51:3; Zechariah 10:7
God as Challenger	Deuteronomy 20:4; 1 Corinthians 15:57
God as Peacemaker	Psalms 85:8; Isaiah 9:6; 52:7; Matthew 5:9

So, discovering your relational pattern is not simply about figuring out your personality, but about finding the marks of the Creator in the amazing jigsaw puzzle that is you. As noted above, the Enneagram relational patterns are about something much more profound than personality. Through these relational patterns we can uncover our deepest fears and desires. Nearly all human behavior is, at its most basic level, the outgrowth of one of these two motivators. And, this is where personality gives way to essence. We might say that a person who is resistant to change is stubborn (a personality trait). But the core of resistance is typically fear. It might be the fear of being rejected or the fear of being betrayed. It might be the fear of being deemed unlovable. Whatever the reason, it's fear just the same. We could say the same thing about desire. A person who tends to take charge of situations may be described as aggressive (a personality trait). Yet, at the core of that aggression is a desire for something—control, love, and security.

The Enneagram identifies the basic fears of the nine relational patterns as follows:

Relational Pattern	Fear
One	Fear of being bad, corrupt, evil, or defective
Two	Fear of being unworthy of being loved
Three	Fear of being worthless or without inherent value
Four	Fear of being without identity or personal significance
Five	Fear of being useless, incapable, or incomplete
Six	Fear of being without support of guidance
Seven	Fear of being deprived or trapped in pain
Eight	Fear of being harmed or controlled by others
Nine	Fear of losing connection or being fragmented

The basic desires for the nine relational patterns are:

Relational Pattern	Desire
One	Desire to have integrity
Two	Desire to be loved
Three	Desire to be valuable
Four	Desire to be oneself
Five	Desire to be competent
Six	Desire to be secure
Seven	Desire to be happy
Eight	Desire to protect oneself
Nine	Desire to be at peace

Read over these lists and consider the fears and desires of your relational pattern. Recognizing these motivators certainly doesn't explain everything about who you are, but it can point to what drives you. You may begin to see yourself through a new lens. Because we tend to act from these fears and desires, being able to identify them is powerful. There's value in seeing how they might be irrational or misplaced. Think of all the terrible dating relationships you could have avoided if you'd known you were just looking for someone to make you feel secure or loved or protected or whatever your basic desire might be. When we pay attention to *why* we do what we do, suddenly we free ourselves to make the choices we *want* to make. We no longer feel compelled to make choices based on some old dance. The developers of the Enneagram point out that, "The Enneagram does not put us in a box, it shows us the box we are already in—and the way out" (Riso and Hudson 1999, 28).

Talk It Over

Now that you have determined your relational pattern, talk with your co-parent about the ways in which you see your relational pattern playing out in your life.

- How well do you fit the general description of your relational pattern?

- In what ways do you differ from this description?

- What other relational patterns do you see in yourself?

- In what ways do the various characteristics of your relational pattern help you function in a healthy way? In what ways do they keep you from functioning in a healthy way?

Look at the list of fears and desires again. If you are still unsure of your Enneagram relational pattern, these might help you zero in on one. Talk with your co-parent about the ways you find yourself acting out of the fear or desire of your relational pattern.

- What is your sense about how you are motivated by the basic fear of your relational pattern? The basic desire?

- Talk about a decision you have made recently based on your basic fear or your basic desire. How would knowing more about yourself have helped you make a different decision?

- In what ways do your basic fears and desires compliment or conflict with those of your co-parent?

- Move back into the larger group and talk together about ideas for working through your fears and desires. Share your thoughts on where these motivators might come from and the kinds of messages you need to hear to work through them.

✠ Your Self and Your Relationships ✠

Learning more about who you are and how you understand yourself can be a fascinating process. But at the end of the day, self-knowledge is only useful if it helps you create stronger, more meaningful relationships with those around you. This includes your co-parent and your children, as well as your family of origin.

As you explore your self-concept, you may find that you uncover something the Enneagram refers to as a "lost childhood message." The Enneagram doesn't focus on the origins of the relational patterns. It does recognize, though, that our families of origin and our childhood experiences impact the relational pattern that emerges in each person. Of course, it's never a good idea to lay a blanket of blame on your family of origin, tempting though it might be. However, legitimate connections often exist between our early family-life experiences and the people we become as adults.

The Enneagram points out that these lost messages have a clear connection to our basic fears and desires. Look carefully at the list below. Keep in mind that the idea that these messages were "lost" doesn't necessarily mean they weren't sent, but rather that they weren't adequately received.

Relational Pattern	Message
One	"You are good."
Two	"You are wanted."
Three	"You are loved for yourself."
Four	"You are seen for who you are."
Five	"Your needs are not a problem."
Six	"You are safe."
Seven	"You will be taken care of."
Eight	"You will not be betrayed."
Nine	"Your presence matters."

When these messages are lost, we seek out relationships that fill in the blanks. A person who lost the message of security—relational pattern Six—will have a greater need for loyalty from her friends and romantic partners. This might not matter as much to a relational pattern Four.

Carlos was the younger of two kids. His older sister, Carmen, was a wild child who got into trouble quite a bit. Carlos often watched his parents fight with Carmen when she was around and complain about her when she wasn't. He rarely saw them treat Carmen with compassion or care. Rather, there seemed to be nothing but tension and distrust in the relationship between Carmen and her parents. Carlos frequently heard his mother speak very critically of Carmen, calling her "no good," "an embarrassment," and a "lousy" kid. Carlos's father, while not openly critical, rarely came to Carmen's defense. Instead, he tended to agree with his wife's assessment of Carmen's character.

As he watched the way his parents dealt with Carmen, Carlos came to believe that it was entirely possible that any misstep on his part would cost him his parents' love. He believed that the best way to make sure his parents continued to love him was to please them with his behavior. He chose to be the opposite of his sister in every way he could.

As an adult, Carlos has unconsciously continued this pattern of people pleasing. He will often refuse to stand up for himself at work, and he has been passed over for promotions that he should have received. In his marriage, Carlos tends to fawn over his wife, Louisa, and avoid conflict by passively agreeing to her choices. He accedes to Louisa's wishes in the movies they see, the way their home is decorated, and where they go on vacation. Carlos frequently finds himself secretly stewing over the way Louisa and his coworkers take advantage of him. But he worries that speaking up about his frustrations will result in more problems both at home and at work.

According to Family Systems language, there are echoes of fusion—that tendency to react to family messages—at work here. Carlos's basic fear is that he will be found unworthy of love. This fear is connected to the messages of his childhood, where love was withheld in the face of misbehavior. In response to this message, Carlos now subverts his real needs and desires so he can be found worthy of love. This is true even at his job, where "love" comes in the form of getting along with coworkers and being seen as a good guy. Because Carlos is acting out of a fear connected with his family of origin, we can say that he is demonstrating fusion.

For Carlos the work of gaining a clearer understanding of himself will involve reclaiming his lost childhood message: "You are loved for yourself." He will also need to recognize the way losing this message supports his fears and confounds his desires. Only when he sees that he is acting out of fear will he be ready to break out of his unhealthy patterns of behavior. By confronting his own fear, Carlos can begin to break the fusion and differentiate from his family of origin. This will be a crucial step toward developing authentic relationships with his wife and his coworkers, not to mention his parents and his sister.

It can be helpful for you to focus on that word "authentic" as you think about your understanding of yourself and how you relate to other people. We all long for authentic relationships. We all want to be loved and accepted for who we are, not for who we think we should be. This has obvious benefits in marriage (something you will explore in the next chapter), but it can also be a crucial step in healing relationships between family members.

Most of us can only get so far in developing a healthy sense of ourselves without addressing the impact of our lost childhood messages. Only when we deal with that loss can we remove the unhealthy patterns associated with it. Then we can move into a place of mutual interdependence within our relationships. This interdependence is the key to developing healthy emotional attachments and patterns of behavior. Only this will allow each of us to be our authentic selves in the dynamic dance that we call family.

Imagine the healing that could take place in Carlos's life if he were to talk with his parents about the way he felt as a child.

In all likelihood they would assure him that they did and still do love him and will continue to do so no matter what. They might even be able to give him a different perspective of their feelings for his sister. Perhaps Carlos only heard their raging. He may never have seen the way they grieved her choices in private. And he may not have heard the conversations between Carmen and his parents where they assured her of their love.

They may respond in a different way. They may tell Carlos he's being ridiculous, or they might admit that they did have a hard time loving his sister. In either case, Carlos will have taken a huge step toward authenticity simply by being honest about his feelings and the way they affect him as an adult. Any change that one family member makes, such as sharing rather than hiding feelings, causes the entire family system to adjust. This, in turn, changes the steps of the family's dance.

Some of this work may be difficult, particularly if you have a strained relationship with your family of origin. Even in a close-knit family, addressing your lost messages and their impact on your sense of yourself can make for an awkward conversation. You don't have to force this. You might not even have to say anything out loud. You might be able to gain perspective on your fears and desires simply by trying to see your family through new eyes. If your basic fear is that you will be found unworthy of love, take the time to think about the ways your family has shown you love. If your fear is that you will be betrayed, think about the ways your family has shown you its loyalty.

At the heart of this process is grace. As children we lack the ability to step outside of ourselves and take an objective view of our relationships. But when we reach adulthood, it becomes a bit easier to set our gut reactions and impulses aside long enough to see our families with a bit more perspective. So as you think about your family system—the role you played in that system and the ways your view of yourself have been formed by the system—resist the urge to fall back on the standing story of your family. Challenge the belief that you fought all the time, that your father was a control freak, that your mother was too critical. Instead, try to see your family with the eyes of compassion, grace, and humility. There can be tremendous healing when we recognize our parents as real human beings who tried their best to be good parents. Seeing them from the vantage of adulthood, we can better understand what they may have been thinking and feeling when you were a child.

It also helps to remember that your parents are someone's children and that they brought their own issues into your family system. Perhaps your mother is critical because that's how her mother treated her. Perhaps your father is passive aggressive—he expresses negative feelings, resentment, and aggression in an unassertive passive way—because he never saw his parents deal with conflict in a productive way. This is where your genogram project will help you gain a new understanding of your family dance and the roles played by all involved. As you see the dynamics behind your family relationships, you'll find stores of grace and understanding you never knew you had.

This is also where you can make room for forgiveness in your relationships. It's easy to start by assigning blame when you think about how your family of origin impacted your view of yourself. Hurtful memories, lost opportunities, even years of depression may lead you to a knee-jerk negative reaction to your family. You may want to dump all of your life's problems on the family that seemed to have caused those problems. But this process is not meant as vindication or revenge for long-standing wrongs. It is, instead, intended to help you understand who you are, that is, the you who participates in your family dance. The best way to move forward is to address the pains of the past, seek healing where you can, and extend grace and forgiveness for the ways in which others hurt you—either intentionally or unintentionally.

This isn't always easy. You will need God's help to step away from what may be years of built-up hurt, anger, or resentment.

But God asks us to show mercy to each other. In Zechariah 7:9, we read, "This is what the Lord Almighty said: 'Administer true justice; show mercy and compassion to one another.'" God's desire for us is that we let go of the hurts of the past and embrace the hopes of the future. We can only do this when we work to live in reconciled relationships with those who have wronged us.

In some cases, reconciliation might require the help of a trained therapist. Here again, if you struggle to make peace with someone in your family, or if you feel pain that seems too big to forgive, talk with your group facilitator about resources that can help. It may take many years and lots of tears to find compassion for someone who hurt you, but doing so may be the best way for you to find the healing and hope you need to move forward. Although Paul was addressing the church, his words also apply to families: "Be kind to one another, tenderhearted, forgiving one another, as God in Christ has forgiven you. Therefore, be imitators of God, as beloved children, and live in love" (Ephesians 4:32–5:2).

This distinction between fixing blame and understanding yourself is especially important as you move into parenting. As a parent you will constantly work to balance your needs and wants against those of your children. For example, recognizing that you have a need for control because you are afraid of being controlled can help you see a situation more clearly. This awareness can free you from acting out of fear and being unnecessarily controlling with your children.

Seeing ourselves as we really are is one of the greatest challenges—and greatest longings—of the human experience. The Scottish poet Robert Burns wrote, "Oh would some power the gift to give us, to see ourselves as others see us." It is no small thing to find the authentic self who lives beneath the layers of fear, doubt, desire, and need that cover us all. But to work toward that end, to uncover the person God created, is perhaps the only goal in life that really matters.

Talk It Over

Think about your family of origin and the lost messages of your child-hood. You may not agree with the message suggested for your type, so don't worry about limiting yourself to that option. Instead, spend some time thinking about where your basic fears and desires might have come from.

- In what ways might your family dance have contributed to your lost message?

- How did your role in the dance reinforce your basic fear and desire?

- How does your lost message impact you in your relationship with your co-parent? With your friends? With your coworkers? With your family of origin?

- Imagine the best relationship you could have with your family of origin. What would need to change for you and your family to move toward that kind of relationship? How can you begin to make that change?

✚ Homework ✚

For this session, your genogram project takes you into some potentially tricky territory. You will be asking your family members to talk about themselves and the messages they received about who they are and their place in the world. You will be trying to identify personal roles and family rules. This might be difficult for some of your family members, particularly those who grew up in a time when therapy and the whole idea of self-examination was unheard of. So tread lightly and be sensitive to the boundaries of each person. Here again, you can get as much information from what someone doesn't say as you can from what they do say.

Genogram—Step 3

1. Do a self-assessment. Take stock of your own role in the family. Where did you fit? What role did you fill? Did you like this role, or did it rub you the wrong way?

2. Describe your perception of your self. What kind of person would you say you are? What pivotal events shaped this self? What overt and covert messages did your family give you that either matched this sense of self or contradicted it?

3. List the various spoken rules that governed your behavior, as well as unspoken rules that may have even more strongly represented things that were taboo or absolute must-dos. Did you tend to obey the rules, bend them, or defiantly break them?

4. Write down your perceptions of the personality traits and roles of your siblings and your parents. This will become a reality check for what you hear them say in your conversations with them.

5. Set up conversations with as many of your immediate family members as are willing and available to talk. Here are some questions to get you started:

   - What was your role in your family?
   - Did you choose that role or was it given to you?
   - How did you feel about that role?
   - Did your role ever change? If so, what brought about the change?
   - Who was the leader in your family, the person who set the tone for how things were done and what was expected?
   - What are some of the events in your life that shaped your sense of yourself?
   - What messages did you get from your family about who you are?
   - How did those messages line up with the way you thought about yourself?

- How has your sense of yourself changed since you became an adult?
- How did your family encourage your uniqueness? How did they discourage it?

If you have the time, you might also want to share the Enneagram information in this chapter with your family members. Let them look over the questions and determine their relational pattern. Use what you've learned about these relational patterns to shape some additional questions about fears, desires, and lost childhood messages.

6. Given what you learned from and about your family, as well as yourself, indicate on the genogram two things about each individual. Indicate one overarching trait that best describes the person's self-image. Indicate the role that person plays in your family. So, to the left of each square or circle, under the symbol for faith, write one word for self-image and below that another word for the role that person played in the family. And in the lower right-hand corner of the genogram, write "Family Rules," and list the top 3–5 rules that governed the family's interaction.

Figure 10: Genogram Step 3: Individual personality and family roles and rules

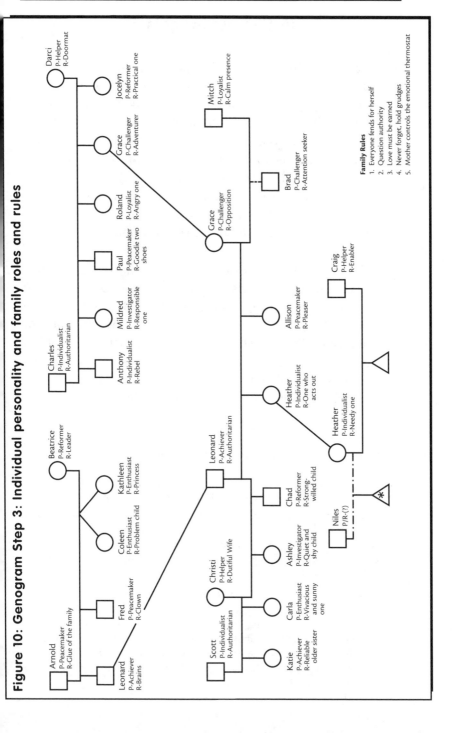

✟ Chapter Insights ✟

1. You are an individual with God-given potential, but the details of your identity—your concept of your self, how you react to things, your desires, etc.—are colored by the dance you do with your family; that is, you are not an island.

2. By identifying your relational pattern through an Enneagram, you equip yourself to anticipate how you will behave or feel given different sets of circumstances. The labels applied to the different relational patterns, and even the relational patterns themselves, are less important than gaining insight into how you perceive and respond to the world around you.

3. Who you are as a person and your role in your family directly affect your relationship with your co-parent and your children. You can shape your family's future to the extent that you freely choose to embrace healthy parts or reject unhealthy parts of your past and present relationships.

4. Forgiveness is an important means for breaking unhealthy relationships and patterns of behavior, as well as healing the personal hurts you have experienced in life.

✟ Resources ✟

Balswick, Jack O., and Judith K. Balswick. *The Family: A Christian Perspective on the Family Home.* Grand Rapids, MI: Baker Academic, 1999.

There are many, many Christian resources that deal with the family, but few do so from the theological, sociological, and psychological perspective the Balswicks offer. Rather than giving pat Christian solutions to the complex challenges of family life, they provide thoughtful, encouraging understanding of how faith and family can intersect.

The Enneagram Institute (http://www.enneagraminstitue.com)

The ideas presented in this chapter only scratch the surface of the Enneagram. If you are interested in taking a more detailed test to determine your relational pattern, you can find several options here. You will also find more complete descriptions of the relational patterns, as well as other tools for exploring the spiritual implications of the Enneagram, and explanations for how various relational patterns interact.

Guest, Judith. *Ordinary People.* New York: Penguin, 1982.

Whether you read the book or watch the 1980 movie starring Donald Sutherland, Mary Tyler Moore, and Timothy Hutton, you will have a hard time finding a better example of the family dance and its impact on self-image.

McGoldrick, Monica. *You Can Go Home Again: Reconnecting with Your Family.* New York: W. W. Norton, 1997.

McGoldrick's book can be a bit academic, but it is an invaluable resource for helping you identify the patterns and factors at work in multiple generations of your family of origin.

Riso, Don Richard, and Russ Hudson. *The Wisdom of the Enneagram.* New York: Bantam, 1999.

The best way to explore the Enneagram relational patterns is to dig into this book, which lays out the complexities and variations of each relational pattern. You will also find out more about the spiritual implications of your relational pattern and the ways in which your understanding of God ties into your general understanding of the world.

The Royal Tenenbaums. Directed by Wes Anderson. Hollywood, CA: Touchstone Pictures, 2001.

This movie delves into the lives of the highly dysfunctional Tenenbaum family, in which each of the adult children suffers under the weight of their parents' expectations. It is a compelling, if exaggerated, take on the way family roles stick.

Satir, Virginia. *The New Peoplemaking.* Los Altos, CA: Science and Behavior, 1988.

This updated version of one of the seminal texts in family therapy is a must read for anyone wanting to understand how families function. Satir's positive outlook and her extensive research with actual families make this book inspiring and extremely insightful.

Chapter 3

Making a Marriage

A successful marriage requires falling in love many times,
always with the same person.

—Mignon McLaughlin

It has been said that there are six people in every marriage: the husband, the wife, and both sets of parents. But a marital relationship is far more crowded than that. People, cultural norms, personal histories, expectations, ideologies, dreams, desires, and even disappointments all play a part. Even those who aren't married bear the marks of the marriages of their parents, siblings, extended families, and friends. Developing a healthy view of marriage, then, involves a whole lot more than getting to know your spouse. It involves a concerted effort to understand the ways all of these other influences color your perspective on marriage.

If you are married, this effort becomes even more important as you and your marriage partner or future co-parent venture into parenthood. The arrival of a child is a blessing. But having children places tremendous demands on a marriage. A child changes the two-person family into a three-person family; overnight you have become a triangle relationship. Children require huge amounts of time, energy, patience, and attention. Dr. John Gottman is a nationally recognized expert on marriage. He notes that 40 to 70 percent of couples experience stress, profound conflict, and a drop in satisfaction with their relationship once the demands of parenting kick in (see http://www.gottman.com). The couples that weather this change best, says Gottman, are those who had a strong and solid friendship before they became parents.

The value of this friendship can't be underestimated. It's what God had in mind when God created human beings. The Bible tells us that God created a man to watch over all of creation. But God saw right away that this man needed a companion, a partner. God said, "It is not good for the man to be alone" (Genesis 2:18). So God created a woman to work with the man and join him in caring for the earth. We all go through life with the desire to connect with other people. We long to be known and loved and accepted for who we are. God created us to be in intimate, meaningful relationships. That's why marriage is such a precious gift from God, one that is worth tending to and preserving.

As you are discovering, much of what you bring to a relationship—a friendship, the parent-child relationship, a marriage—is influenced by the family in which you grew up. This session, then, will focus on the ways your family of origin shaped your beliefs about marriage. It will help you gain a better understanding of the assumptions you bring to your relationship with your co-parent. It will help you build the kind of strong, stable friendship you need to make the transition into parenthood.

✠ Facing Reality ✠

There is a great deal of talk these days about the fragile state of marriage in our culture. Politicians and pastors alike often cite the statistic that anywhere from 40 to 50 percent of marriages end in divorce. This is typically attributed to a variety of social forces: a decline in moral vaules among the current generation, the media's tendency to create false expectations of romance and marriage, or our society's obsession with sex. There may very well be some credence to these claims. But the truth is that cultural forces play only a small part in our ideas about marriage and relationships.

Studies suggest that the way adults perceive their parents' marriage has the most influence on what they themselves expect of marriage. These perceptions become their blueprint for how to treat—and be treated by—a spouse. That doesn't mean you are destined to have a marriage exactly like your parents'. Rather, it suggests that your most basic ideas about marriage come from your impressions of your parents' relationship.

This is where what you're learning about Family Systems Theory (FST) comes in handy. Much of what you believe about marriage is based on the roles you may have assigned to your parents, the story you tell about their relationship, and the conscious and unconscious messages you picked up about marriage. The more realistic your perception of your parents' relationship is, the more likely you are to build a resilient relationship yourself.

A study from the University of Texas at Austin found that when it comes to assessing their parents' marriage, adults tend to fall into one of three categories:

- *Secure* adults are able to offer a balanced, believable assessment of their parents' marriage.
- *Dismissing* adults tend to minimize or discount the negative effects of childhood experiences, either by saying they can't recall some childhood events or by idealizing their parents.
- *Preoccupied* adults are unable or unwilling to talk about negative childhood experiences and instead change the subject or talk about their family of origin in vague generalities.

The researchers used these categories to assess the effects of having children on couples' marriages. They found that both *dismissing* adults and *preoccupied* adults paid less attention to their marriages once they became parents. The dismissing adults seemed to continue to deny the importance of childhood experiences and often denied problems in their own marriages as well. They were unable or unwilling to acknowledge the increased stress in their marriages after children entered the family. Naturally, this pattern of dismissing will make it difficult for these adults to deal with the conflict and stress that come with being parents.

The *preoccupied* adults, on the other hand, initially put more work into their marriages once children arrived. These couples reportedly feared that the relationship would suffer. Behind the scenes, it became apparent that unresolved issues from their childhood really drove the preoccupied adults to this extra effort. In other words, their work on the marriage was an attempt to deal with unacknowledged negative childhood experiences. Eventually the preoccupied adults decreased the amount of work they put into their marriages because the work didn't accomplish the goal of relieving their fears.

As you have probably guessed, the secure adults fared best in this study, though not for the reasons you might expect. The secure adults didn't necessarily all have ideal childhoods or positive models of marriage. In fact, the study found that the key to making a relatively smooth transition to parenting was for the adults involved to have a *realistic* understanding of their parents' marriage, regardless of how good or bad that marriage was. As the authors of the study reported in the June 2005 issue of the *Journal of Family Psychology*, "Memories of a negative parental marriage do not predict low maintenance or declines in maintenance across the transition to parenthood but rather, lacking access to these memories or denying their importance, predict problems with maintenance. It may be that rich memories of a disharmonious parental marriage offer the best preparation for dealing with the stresses presented by family transitions."

Gaining a more realistic view of your parents' relationship can have some surprising ripple effects. As you begin to see each of your parents in a new light, you begin to see yourself—in a parenting role—more realistically. While this is part of the goal of exploring your family of origin, it can be a difficult and disconcerting process.

Mark remembers his parents fighting on a regular basis. Their arguments often turned vicious. Both his mother and father allowed their emotions to escalate to a point just short of violence. As a child, Mark believed these arguments were mostly his father's fault. Mark's mother often spoke about her husband in negative terms. This was partly out of her intense frustration and anger at him. It was also her attempt to make her children see him as the villain and her as the victim. As Mark took in these messages from his mother, he became emotionally distant from his father.

As an adult, however, Mark has come to see that his parents shared responsibility for their often-volatile relationship. After years of feeling like an outsider in the family, Mark's father began to make a concerted effort to connect with his children. As Mark slowly grew closer to his father, he saw how his father tried to relate to Mark's mother. Mark began to see that his mother was often the instigator of conflict. Mark realized that she typically met her husband's efforts to be close to her with either the cold shoulder or anger.

Mark certainly saw the ways his father contributed to the problems between himself and Mark's mother. At the same time, he came to realize that their issues were not nearly as one-sided as he had once believed.

This revelation led Mark to some serious soul searching. For most of his life, Mark had thought there were always a right side and a wrong side in a conflict. When he had a problem with his wife, his friends, or his coworkers, Mark often dug in. He would be unwilling to concede that the other party might have a valid perspective on the subject at hand. As Mark developed this new understanding of his parents' marriage, he recognized that, like his mother, he had the propensity to blame others exclusively for problems. Gradually, he became more willing to consider his part in a conflict.

Mark had long thought of himself as his mother's protector. He had been her champion, her trusted ally in the fight against his father.

As Mark reconnected with his father, Mark saw how painful it had been for him to be the "enemy" in the eyes of his children. Mark was able to consider how he would feel in his father's shoes. In the end, Mark was truly sorry for the way he'd treated his father. He found himself grieving the relationship with his father that he'd missed out on because of the messages he'd received from his mother.

Mark also found himself growing more and more angry with his mother for her part in turning him against his father. Whenever he spent time with his parents, Mark became increasingly aware of her attempts to manipulate his feelings. This perspective on his mother was deeply troubling for Mark. He was used to thinking about her as the put-upon wife and mother. He had a difficult time reconciling his new understanding of her part in the family system with his long-standing sense of loyalty to her.

Like most people, Mark had a set of assumptions about his parents' relationship. These were based on his experiences as a child. They were also based on direct and indirect messages from his parents themselves. The assumptions we make about the relationships we saw in our family of origin are at the center of how we think about marriage and relationships as adults.

As you think about your parents' relationship, remember that nothing in a family system stands in isolation. Your parents came to their marriage with their own individual expectations. These were patterned on the marriages of your maternal and paternal grandparents. As you work to gain a more realistic perspective on your parents' relationship, consider what you've discovered in the process of creating your genogram.

When Shanti was growing up, she rarely saw her parents interact. Shanti's dad worked hard and didn't do much with the family, something that her mother often complained about. Shanti and her siblings grew up with the sense that their dad wasn't very interested in them. He became a kind of outsider within the family.

It wasn't until Shanti started working on a genogram for a class that she saw her father in a new light. While interviewing her dad, she learned that her paternal grandfather had been married to someone else before he married her grandmother. Her paternal grandmother was much younger than Shanti's grandfather. Their marriage was the subject of all kinds of gossip in the small town where her father grew up. In an effort to stay above the fray, Shanti's grandparents kept to themselves. As a result, they had a very limited social circle and Shanti's father had only a few friends. The message he got from his parents was that other people were not necessarily trustworthy, that it was better to keep to yourself and not risk having people turn against you. Shanti's father responded to this message by becoming a very private person. This made it hard for him to develop warm, trusting relationships with his wife and children.

It would be easy for Shanti to assume that her father's difficulty with intimacy is the source of the relationship issues in her family of origin. But such an assumption would be both unfair and unhelpful. If Shanti truly wants to understand her parents' relationship she needs to think of her parents as individuals with unique histories that are essential to her total assessment of her family of origin.

This exploration into the ways your family of origin shaped your ideas about relationships and marriage may be one of the richest veins you will mine in this course. You could easily spend the next three sessions talking exclusively about the connections between your family of origin and your relationship with your co-parent. Those messages influence everything from how you express your emotions, to your feelings about sex, to your views on the importance of work and money.

While you could—and perhaps should—dig into those specific issues more deeply at some point, you will have a difficult time making headway without addressing one core element of marriage: conflict. Every marriage, every relationship, involves conflict. Knowing how to navigate the rough waters of an argument or hurt feelings and choose forgiveness instead of revenge are at the center of developing a marriage that can survive the impact of children.

Talk It Over

Spend some time alone thinking about your parents' relationship. Keep in mind that the goal of this exercise is to recall realistic pictures of your parents' relationship, not idealized memories or dark distortions.

- Think of a time when you saw your parents working as a team. What do you remember about the way they treated each other? Was this kind of interaction common or unusual?

- Try to remember a time when you saw your parents in conflict. How did they treat each other in this situation? If you don't remember your parents arguing, consider why that might be the case. Did they hide their conflict or avoid conflict? Why do you think they dealt with conflict the way they did?

- What family situations seemed to stress your parents? What situations seemed to bring them joy or pleasure?

- What messages did your mother give you about your father? What messages did your father give you about your mother? Do you think these messages were accurate?

Once you've worked through these questions on your own, share your thoughts with your co-parent. Talk together about some of the implications your parents' relationship has for your relationship with each other.

✛ Fightin' Words ✛

Remember when you were young and you imagined what it would be like to be in love? You may have pictured yourself holding hands with your beloved. You may have fantasized about long walks on the beach or the magical connection you'd feel when you met "The One." But did you ever dream about the man or woman with whom you could fight?

If you've spent more than a half a day with your co-parent, you have probably run into some kind of conflict. We don't like to think about fighting with someone we love. But every relationship involves conflict—have you ever had one without it? Certainly, as demanding and stressful as marriage is, conflict is inevitable. Imagine the conflict that existed in Isaac and Rebekah's marriage (Genesis 27). But many of us grew up with the exact opposite message—that conflict is bad, that you don't argue with someone you love, that couples who really care about each other never have problems. The way your family of origin handled—or didn't handle—conflict and the impact that had on you may be one of the most fundamental issues to come up in marriage.

Sam grew up in a family where his parents fought much of the time. Sam's wife, Alicia, grew up in a family with very little open conflict. When Sam and Alicia started dating, they talked about their families and how different they were. Once they actually spent time with each other's families, the differences became obvious. Sam was astounded that a family could get along so well. Alicia was taken aback to see Sam's folks argue openly in front of them.

It didn't take long for the differences in their families to show up in Sam and Alicia's relationship. After they had dated for several months, Sam and Alicia started talking about getting married. Alicia was hesitant. In her mind, she and Sam argued far too much for them to have a good life together. It didn't seem normal to her for two people who said they loved each other to disagree so often and so vocally. From Sam's perspective, however, he and Alicia were doing great! He thought they had a wonderful relationship, one that allowed them both to be honest about their feelings even when they disagreed.

For both Sam and Alicia, the families in which they grew up influenced their expectations of how much conflict was "normal."

You may find that this is an area where it's difficult to get a realistic picture of your family of origin. There are plenty of generational, cultural, and religious issues tied in with the subject of conflict. If you grew up with stoic parents, you may have a hard time remembering anything that resembled conflict in your family. Or perhaps you come from a family where emotions are always openly exressed and intense, and it's hard to know if someone is upset or just excited. As you work through the rest of this chapter, do your best to create an overall picture of the conflict patterns in your family of origin.

Your approach to conflict won't only have an impact on your relationship with your co-parent. It will affect your relationship with your children as well. Conflict between you and your co-parent was one thing before your child arrived—a two-person conflict, with its own set of how you might respond to and resolve the conflict. When a child enters a family unit of two (or dyad), the family becomes a threesome (or triad). And with a third person in the mix, the two people in conflict now can pull the third person into the conflict, which makes it a triangle. While you both may love your child, the relationship triangle between you, your co-parent, and your children can be a source of conflict. (See Appendix A for a more in-depth discussion of the FST concept of relationship triangles.) If you have a tendency to yell at the people who upset you, you'll need to consider if that is the approach you want to take when your children upset you. If you are someone who doesn't like to argue, you'll need to think about how you'll handle the inevitable arguments with your children. These kinds of issues can only be addressed when you have a firm sense of the deeper implications of your family's influence on your conflict style.

Talk It Over

Consider the messages about conflict, emotions, and forgiveness you saw modeled in the relationships around you. Talk with your co-parent about the impact of these messages on your relationship.

- How often did you see your parents argue? How would you describe the tone of their arguments?

- What messages did you take away from your parents' conflict style?

- Did anyone in your family hold a grudge against someone else in the family? How was that grudge addressed? What did this situation teach you about how to deal with conflict?

- In what ways does your conflict style reflect the way conflict was handled in your family of origin?

- Discuss a recent conflict where you feel you and your co-parent handled the situation in a healthy, productive way.

- Now discuss a recent conflict that left one or both of you feeling hurt or angry. What can you learn from these two experiences?

- What conflict skills do you feel you need to develop in order to have a healthy approach to conflict in your relationship with your co-parent?

Fusion

Both the level and tone of relationship conflict are related to our families of origin. There is not necessarily a one-to-one correlation between quantity and intensity of conflict. In fact, this is an area where people often react to their family of origin through fusion. You'll recall that fusion is the way in which people remain connected to the emotional, behavioral, religious, and other patterns of their family, either by repeating the pattern (positive fusion) or by doing the exact opposite (negative fusion). The first step in establishing an approach to conflict that works for you and your co-parent is to recognize the places of fusion in your assumptions about conflict.

> Miko grew up in a family where strong emotions were frowned upon. When Miko cried or got angry or upset, her mother would offer a bit of comfort. Still, she was quick to try to contain Miko's feelings, saying, "That's enough," when she thought Miko should be finished with her emotional response to a situation. Miko rarely saw her parents disagree and never saw them argue or fight. In Miko's world, strong emotions were a sign of personal weakness. Mature people knew how to control their feelings and deal with them internally. Miko learned to believe in being placid and stoic. She carried this belief into adulthood and into her marriage with Hiroshi.
>
> Miko sometimes disagreed with Hiroshi about decisions and often felt anger or frustration toward him. Even so, she usually kept these feelings to herself. At least she thought she did. In reality, Miko's emotions found their way out through sarcasm and passive aggression. If Hiroshi didn't unload the dishwasher when it was his turn, Miko would put the dishes away herself. Her feelings were "expressed" by the slamming cupboard doors and the rattling plates. If Hiroshi questioned her about her behavior, she would snidely deny being upset. She secretly hoped he'd get the message that she was angry and that he would change his behavior.

Miko's behavior was a response to the messages she had received growing up: Anger is not acceptable. "Negative" feelings need to be bottled up. Mature people don't argue. Miko exemplifies positive fusion, handling difficult emotions in very much the same way as her parents. A person who grows up in a family like Miko's could also react to the closed-off emotions of the family by becoming a hyper-emotional person (negative fusion). This negative fusion might become manifest as lashing out in anger at the slightest provocation, or as a tendency to escalate conflict quickly and disproportionately. An example might be Cain's reaction and behavior in Genesis 4. Both kinds of fusion—positive and negative—get in the way of dealing with conflict in a productive way.

Fusion, both the negative and positive types, makes it difficult for you and your co-parent to develop patterns of conflict that reflect the kind of relationship you want to have. This is where you need to pay close attention to the patterns you see in your family of origin and make conscientious decisions to choose which ones you want to carry into your family life.

Cutoff

At its most extreme, fusion can result in something called *cutoff*. Cutoff happens when we sever ourselves from undesirable feelings and experiences or from unpleasant relationships. Often a person cuts herself off from a relationship by never having contact, perhaps moving far away and not responding to phone messages, e-mail, or letters. There may be an uncle no one talks to or who simply isn't invited to family gatherings. The shared understanding is that "he wouldn't want to come anyway." Or maybe you or one of your siblings intentionally moved far away from the rest of the family to avoid dealing with that relationship. Look at how Jacob cut himself off from his brother Esau in Genesis 27–28. You might talk on the phone or even have an occasional visit, but, for the most part, little connects you outside of a sense of obligation.

Sometimes a cutoff is strictly emotional. A brother might refuse to engage in any kind of emotional connection with his sister, even though they see each other regularly and attend the same church. In this case, a cutoff reflects the absence of genuine emotional connections between people. Grandma Annie and Aunt Liz may be capable of being in the same room, but they are incapable of actually talking to each other about anything of substance. And if they do talk, each feels the emotional chill in the air.

These cutoffs often get passed down through families from one generation to the next—Aunt Liz's children may inherit their mother's touchy relationship with their grandmother. Because of the cutoff between Grandma and Mom, the children never develop a relationship with their grandmother. They therefore extend the cutoff to the next generation. These children may grow up and never determine for themselves if they want to have a relationship with their grandmother.

Cutoff may sound like the exact opposite of fusion, but they are actually closely related. In most cases, a cutoff is a reaction to the family of origin. It is an extreme way of dealing with a deep, usually painful, relationship. The link between cutoff and fusion is that both are responses to something that happens in the relationship—they are *re*actions, not a genuine *action* that grows out of a person's authentic sense of themselves and what they want. If you kick your leg when a doctor taps your knee with an instrument, that's a reaction, whereas, if you kick your leg because you are doing a cheerleading routine, that's an action.

It's important to identify the places of fusion and cutoff in your family of origin because they carry over into your relationship with your co-parent in some subtle, deeply harmful ways. For example, a wife might have a difficult time hearing the emotional needs of her husband because no one in her family expressed emotions directly. The positive fusion she has with her family of origin can lead her to a "you're weird because that's not the way we did it" mentality. This kind of response can leave her spouse feeling isolated and ignored.

Many couples use cutoff as a means of manipulating each other. Look at how David employed cutoff against his wife Michal (2 Samuel 6). This is particularly true for adults who grew up in families where cutoff was a common step in conflict. In marriage, cutoff might look like days of silence or even the threat of moving out. This kind of extreme emotional response is not one people come up with on their own. More often, it is a reflection of the family of origin. Overcoming these family patterns is no small task. If you and your co-parent find you are stuck in a cycle of arguing, hurt feelings, and unresolved issues, this is a great time to consider couples counseling. Once your child arrives, it will be far more difficult for you to find the time—not to mention the energy— to dig into your relationship with the kind of intentionality that can help you develop a stronger relationship.

✛ Fighting Fair ✛

It's one thing to recognize the influence of your family of origin in your conflicts with your co-parent. It's another thing to try to develop new patterns and ways of thinking about and handling conflict—old, multigenerational habits die hard. But as you're discovering, doing so has benefits that go far beyond helping the two of you get along. Creating and modeling effective, respectful methods for handling conflict might be one of the greatest gifts you can give to your child.

The key to creating new patterns is recognizing the patterns that don't work. And it's good to do that before you are in the midst of an argument. It can be hard to step back from the strong emotions in a conflict situation. Seriously, verbal guns blazing away, who is capable of saying, "Wait a minute, am I reacting in a way that reflects my real feelings or am I just following the pattern of my family of origin?" So take time to recognize and resolve unhelpful patterns now, when you're calm and motivated to make a change. Then, when you and your co-parent find yourselves in the middle of the next spat, you'll have new tools that will help you resolve the problem more effectively. You will still have conflict, only now you will be equipped to resolve the conflict in a healthy fashion.

Healthy conflict involves following a few basic ground rules. Facing conflict, particularly conflict in a marriage, often brings you quickly to the fine line between honesty and cruelty. Too often we use arguments as an excuse to dump all of our frustrations, anger, and backlog of score to settle on our unsuspecting partner. Chances are you've had at least one fight where one of you did something that was meant to hurt the other person. Some clear rules can help you resolve the issue at hand like civilized people.

From a family systems perspective, the biggest temptation in conflict is to create triangles. Remember, couples create triangles in an effort to diffuse tension. Note how Abram and Sarai, for instance, pulled Hagar into their relationship to form a triangle (Genesis 16). Pairs in conflict pull other people or things into the middle of the relationship to take some of the heat off of the couple. But most of the time, triangles make things worse.

Vanessa and Jamaal have been married for three years. Jamaal was recently promoted at his job and has started working longer hours in an effort to keep up with his new responsibilities. At first, Vanessa was thrilled for Jamaal. She was happy for the extra income and supported his need to work extra hours. On occasion, she'd bring him dinner so they could spend a little more time together during his long days. After several months, however, Vanessa started to feel like Jamaal was spending more time at work because he wanted to, not because he had to. She knew he liked the feeling of power he got at work. He had people who reported to him and who did what he asked them to do without question. She got the impression that life at home with her felt boring in comparison.

One night Jamaal got home just as Vanessa was going to bed. She lashed out at him, telling him that she was sick of his new job. She went on to accuse him of letting his work, not his commitment to the family, dictate his priorities. Needless to say, the conversation didn't go well. Exhausted and frustrated after a long day, Jamaal accused Vanessa of not being supportive. He wished she could see that he needed to put in the extra time so that they could have a better life together. After an hour of heated arguing they went to bed, both of them feeling hurt and angry, with nothing resolved.

In Jamaal and Vanessa's case, Jamaal's work had become the third corner of a triangle. Vanessa's real concern was that Jamaal was bored with her. She was scared that she was losing his attention and affection. But instead of talking with Jamaal about these genuine feelings, she blamed his work for the tension she felt with him.

Jamaal had also allowed his work to create a triangle, but in a different way. Jamaal had indeed used his job as a way of feeling more important and adding some excitement to his life. He enjoyed feeling needed and admired. This was something that he used to get from Vanessa, but this had faded over time. So, like Vanessa, Jamaal pulled a new member into the triangle, rather than deal directly with the real issue of his lack of fulfillment. What he really needed was not the new job but a renewed bond with Vanessa. Until both of them bump the third party out of their relationship, they will have a hard time getting to the root of their conflict. That doesn't mean Jamaal has to quit his job. It just means Jamaal and Vanessa need to acknowledge that the job isn't the issue. They need to see the job as a symptom of the issue.

In some cases, the metaphorical ghost of someone from our past ends up playing the third corner. It might be an old boyfriend with a hot temper. It might be a passive-aggressive mother, or a grandparent who controlled the family with manipulative guilt trips. It might even be a fear that we are repeating patterns from the family of origin. An equally obvious way that triangles form is through one of the persons having an affair. Think of what gave rise to the triangle between Bathsheba, Uriah, and David (2 Samuel 11). The results can turn out deadly.

Review the example about Miko and Hiroshi above. Miko's family pattern of repressed emotion has taken on a life of its own. This pattern itself is preventing Miko and Hiroshi from addressing the real issues that exist between them. Miko's difficulties in expressing her emotions certainly need to be addressed. But it would be easy for Hiroshi to blame these difficulties for all of the problems that arise in their marriage. It would be convenient for Hiroshi to use this issue as a means of deflecting responsibility for making their marriage work.

Our Arsenal of Weapons

Creating triangles is just one of the many coping strategies we use to manage conflict. There are plenty of other weapons we pull out when we're fighting with someone we care about. These include avoidance, blame, bringing up the past, and holding a grudge.

Avoidance: Some of us have learned that the best way to handle disagreement is to pretend it never happened and just move on. In the Bible, Moses went to great lengths to avoid his grandfather by adoption, Pharaoh (Exodus 2:15). This can actually be a healthy choice from time to time. Avoidance isn't, however, a sustainable approach to conflict because it can just defer and fuel an even bigger blow-up in your relationship. In the long run, it's more effective to work through issues together toward a mutual resolution.

Blame: David Augsburger says, "It is of little value to fix blame. . . . It takes two to have a problem" (Augsburger 1981, 12). Often, one co-parent is reluctant to accept his or her part in a conflict, particularly if that person feels like the wronged party. But there is nearly always a need for shared responsibility. The blame game was originally invented by Adam and Eve in the Garden of Eden (Genesis 3), so ridding ourselves of that response is no easy task.

Bringing up the past: This tried-and-true technique is hard to resist. It feels good—at least in the moment—to unload all of your pent-up frustrations in the midst of one big argument. But it is far more effective to focus solely on the issue at hand. Now the issue might be the tip of a bigger iceberg, but it's important to stick to what is happening now, not what happened four months ago. Who can forget how the older brother responded when the prodigal son returned home in Jesus' parable (Luke 15:25–32)? If you didn't bring it up then, it's not fair to bring it up now. If you did bring it up then and found some kind of resolution, it's not fair to make your co-parent keep paying for a past mistake.

Holding a grudge: If you've worked through a problem, then let it go. Love each other enough to start again. Too often, couples give lip service to resolution just to make the present discomfort of conflict go away. Both people have a need to talk about what's bothering them and have those feelings heard. If this doesn't happen, then the anger and hurt of the situation are bound to linger. Joseph's brothers feared that he would hold a grudge against them for how they treated him as a youth (Genesis 50:15). Typically such anger and hurt does not get expressed directly. It nonetheless finds its way out in sarcastic comments, sexual rejection, silence, or emotional disconnection.

✠ Four Signs of Trouble ✠

During the past twenty years, John Gottman has studied married couples to determine what helps them stay together and what pulls them apart. Much of his work has focused on conflict. Perhaps his biggest contribution to our understanding of relationships today is his belief that conflict is an inevitable part of marriage. His research shows that the goal of a relationship ought not be to get rid of conflict, but rather to engage in conflict well.

Gottman identifies what he calls the "Four Horsemen of the Apocalypse." These are four signs that a relationship is in trouble. All four have the potential to come out to play in the midst of conflict.

1. Criticism: Constructive conflict focuses on specific behaviors, not character flaws. But criticism is all about a personal attack. Comments like, "I'd like you to pick up your dirty clothes and put them in the laundry basket," are directed at behavior. Comments like, "Why are you such a stupid slob?" are directed at character. These kinds of comments are meant to demean, belittle, and hurt. In Gottman's studies men and women generally dealt with conflict in similar ways. However, one of the few differences is that women were more likely to criticize, whereas men tended to withdraw in the face of conflict because they were less effective when expressing themselves.

2. Contempt: When we turn up the intensity of our criticism, we transform it into contempt. It is an open sign of disrespect.

Contempt can look like sarcasm, sighs or grunts of derision, eye rolling, or even flat-out mockery.

3. Defensiveness: Getting defensive is a natural response to conflict. This is particularly true when you are the offending party. But defensiveness is essentially a move of self-preservation that rarely helps improve the relationship. In fact, it prevents a person from really hearing or processing what the other person is saying. Defensiveness might look like denial of responsibility, instant rebuttals ("Well, you never listen to me either!"), or intense anger.

4. Stonewalling: If you've ever had an argument with someone who simply refuses to respond, you've experienced stonewalling. On rare occasions, this can actually be a healthy response. If, for example, one of you is so upset that you can't think straight, it might be helpful to say, "I can't talk about this with you right now. Let's calm down and come back to it later when we can listen to each other." But routine stonewalling is a way of pulling away from the relationship altogether. Often stonewalling is used as a way of making the other person take the blame for the conflict. It allows one person to act like the "calm" one as opposed to the "hysterical" or "moody" one.

See if you can recognize these four signs of unhealthy ways of responding to conflict in the story of Javier and Lorena.

Javier's wife Lorena has a hard time sticking to their budget. She grew up in a family where financial issues were rarely discussed. If she wanted something, she usually got it. In Javier's family of origin, however, money was always tight and the source of much anxiety. Even though he has a good job and he and Lorena live comfortably, Javier has a hard time believing they will ever be truly secure financially. Javier's fears about money often lead him to lash out at Lorena when it comes time to pay their bills each month.

Rather than just telling Lorena that her spending concerns him, Javier tends to attack Lorena's intelligence. He'll say things like, "I don't know how you can be so stupid!" or "My twelve-year-old sister could keep track of her money better than you can." His demeaning tone and belittling words suggest that he has very little faith in Lorena's ability to be an equal partner in their financial decisions.

Lorena can hardly bear listening to Javier talk about money. Lately, she can hardly bear to listen to him talk at all. Still, Lorena plays a part in making conversations about finances difficult. When these issues began, Lorena dismissed Javier's concerns. And the more he pushed, the less she listened. There have been times when she has spent money she knew she shouldn't just to see how Javier would react. When Javier chides her for spending too much, Lorena often hides her resentment behind a snide laugh.

Javier and Lorena do try to have productive conversations about their financial situation, but because they have fallen into such damaging patterns of conflict, even these conversations quickly degenerate into arguments. Once that happens, it becomes almost impossible for them to communicate effectively. They spend most of their energy trying to lay blame on each other. Javier will tell Lorena she is ruining their future. Lorena will tell Javier she spends money because it's the only thing that makes her happy, because he's a lousy husband. Any love or respect they have for each other is covered up by their anger and defensiveness. They both stubbornly hold onto their positions and become unable to accept responsibility for their parts in the problem.

When Javier gets completely fed up with Lorena, he simply stops talking to her. While Lorena often responds to Javier's criticism with derision, there are times when she shows her hurt and begins to cry. Javier has become so frustrated by this issue that he rarely feels any tenderness toward Lorena. So when Lorena cries, Javier often tells her she's getting "crazy" on him and leaves the room. Rather than step toward his wife in an effort to seek genuine reconciliation, Javier steps away from her—physically and emotionally. This shuts down all possible communication, leaving them both feeling alone and emotionally abandoned.

Every couple will resort to these behaviors at some point. When all four are present and persistent, it's a sign that the relationship is in need of serious help. In fact, Gottman's research suggests that if one person makes an effort to rid the relationship of these behaviors and the other person doesn't, there is a 90 percent chance the relationship will fail.

Talk It Over

Look at the problematic patterns of conflict discussed above. Speak with your co-parent about ways to keep these behaviors from eroding your relationship.

- What are some of the triangles that exist in your relationship? How can you break these and get to the real issues between you?

- Talk about a time when you have used one of the "Four Horsemen" in a conflict. What was your motivation for using this behavior?

- Together, brainstorm other ways you could have resolved that conflict without bringing in one of the Horsemen.

- Think of three long-standing conflicts that keep coming up between the two of you. What new conflict resolution skills could you use to help you move toward resolution on these issues? Some possibilities might be:

  1. Define the problem(s) that spark the conflict.

  2. Focus on one issue at a time.

  3. Restrict your comments to specific behaviors.

  4. Choose each other as teammates to find possible solutions to the problem, rather than viewing your co-parent as on the opposing team.

  5. Agree on a workable solution that will help you deal with the conflicts you will have in the future.

- When one of these conflicts actually happens, stop immediately to give yourselves some time to cool off. Make an appointment with your co-parent to discuss what brought on the conflict. When you sit down to talk, apologize, if that is appropriate; share with each other how the other person's use of the conflict "Horsemen" hurt you; clarify the real underlying issue of the conflict; and write down a promise that you can make to your co-parent, and keep, to prevent that same issue from causing the level of conflict it did in that case.

✠ The Power of Grace ✠

At the core of healthy patterns of conflict is the belief that you and your co-parent are each worthy of respect, compassion, and forgiveness. Too often we let marriage become an excuse for treating our spouse in ways we would never treat our friends. But sharing a life and creating a family with someone involves a kind of selflessness that must supercede our all-too-human need to be right.

The Christian life is based on the belief that Jesus Christ, the Son of God, sacrificed himself for our sake. Even before his death and resurrection, Jesus lived a life of sacrifice and servanthood. Jesus often told his followers that their lives needed to be centered on what they could give, not what they could get. He explained that they were to love others as much as they love themselves (Luke 10:27). But he also explained that doing so would involve loving others even when they were hard to love (Luke 10:30–37). He showed his disciples that he wanted them to live humbly and see themselves as servants to other people. You may recall the story of Jesus washing the feet of his disciples. When he was done, he told them, "Now that I, your Lord and Teacher, have washed your feet, you also should wash one another's feet. I have set you an example that you should do as I have done for you. Very truly I tell you, servants are not greater than their master, nor are messengers greater than the one who sent them" (John 13: 14–16).

So often marriage becomes a battle of wills. We want our needs met, and we can easily slip into subtle games meant to make our spouse do what we want them to do. But true partnership involves letting go of our selfishness. It involves seeing our spouses through the lens of grace.

It's ironic that marriage is both the place we are often at our worst and the place we expect the most from the other person. We can be far too quick to cast blame, to point out faults, to see what's wrong with our spouses. But strong, healthy marriages are those built on forgiveness and grace. The best marriages, and the best families, are those in which everyone feels accepted and loved without condition. But creating that atmosphere of acceptance and love will necessitate putting aside our expectations of perfection in the other person.

It is helpful to keep in mind what you learned about the Enneagram relational patterns in the previous chapter. Once you have a better understanding of your spouse's relational pattern, you will begin to see that the aspects of his or her personality that bother you most might very well be your spouse's attempts at dealing with the fears and desires of his or her relational pattern.

Al and Yanna have been married for four years. For the most part, Yanna thinks the world of Al. But he has a tendency to see the negative side of every situation, and it has started to drive her crazy. They have had a hard time finding a church home because Al can always find something he dislikes about each congregation they attend. He complains about his job so often that Yanna has a hard time mustering up any sympathy for him. They have several other couples they like to spend time with. But each time they drive home from someone's house, Al brings up something about their hosts that bugs him.

Now Yanna is expecting their first child, and she has started to worry that Al will take all the joy out of parenting with his constant negativity. She doesn't want to raise their child in a home filled with complaints. Al and Yanna have started going to couples therapy in hopes of dealing with Yanna's frustration before the baby comes. At one session, the therapist had them work through the Enneagram inventory. Yanna tested as a Nine (The Peacemaker) and Al tested as a One (The Reformer). As they learned more about their relational patterns, Yanna began to understand that what she saw as Al's negativity was an expression of his desire for perfection. What she thought of as complaining, Al thought of as pointing out where something could be made better.

Once Yanna had this perspective on Al's view of the world, she was better able to press him to talk about what he liked about a situation or a person. For his part, Al made an effort to let his need for perfection inspire him to try new ideas. For example, rather than just talking about the ways his job could improve, Al became more proactive in bringing about those improvements.

This is another area where your understanding of family systems can help you move forward into the kind of life you want for your children. Recognizing the importance of grace in the family you are building can help you begin to extend grace to the family from which you came. You don't have to pretend past hurts never took place or that the people you grew up with were perfect. Instead, you can see each person in your family the way you want to be seen by your spouse: as a flawed person trying your best to build meaningful relationships.

As you prepare for parenthood, you will put much of your effort into figuring out how to care for your child emotionally, spiritually, and physically. That's how it should be. Yet more than anything else, your child needs parents who love each other. Children learn valuable lessons from parents who take the time to tend to their relationship, even in the midst of tending to their family. They need parents who forgive each other. Children need parents who can accept them for who they are. It is no small task to maintain a relationship during the transition to parenthood. You will most assuredly run into your share of bumps along the way. But by working though some of the messages about marriage, conflict, and love you inherited from your family of origin, you have made tremendous strides at keeping those bumps from derailing your relationship.

✚ Homework ✚

This week you have the opportunity to discuss with family members memories of marriage and conflict. As you reflect back on these conversations, look for triangles and patterns of fusion and cutoff. Listen to family stories about someone who was or is shut out of the family, either physically or emotionally. If you can, ask follow-up questions about the impact of these cutoffs on other family members. If possible, try to speak with the person who has been cut off to get his or her perspective of the issue. If you find that members of your family have a difficult time talking about conflict or admitting to it, try to uncover the messages they might have received about conflict that have led to this difficulty.

Genogram—Step 4

1. As before, turn your attention inward to begin with. If you are or have been married, what ideals did you have about marriage before you got married? If you are not married and have not been, what ideals do you have about what marriage would be like? In your family of origin, do people view living together as an acceptable alternative, or prelude, to marriage?

2. If you reflect honestly on your own relationship with your co-parent, how would you describe your response to conflict between the two of you? What are the hot-button topics for you? Do you get anxious just thinking of having to talk with your co-parent about a certain issue or problem? Does a particular kind of response from your co-parent really set you off? Would you say that you and your co-parent have no conflicts? Do the two of you prefer to avoid conflict or pretend it is not there?

3. Can you identify any triangles in your relationship with your co-parent? Who or what serves as the third side of the triangle? Why do you think that person, activity, or whatever it is got roped in to play the third-party foil in your relationship? Since having an affair is one extreme form of a triangle, do you know of anyone in your family who has had one or more extramarital affairs? If so, what happened as a result?

4. As you scan the marriages in each generation on your genogram, how would you characterize their response to conflict—your grandparents, parents, or siblings who are in committed relationships? Do the people on your genogram handle conflict in the same way or differently?

5. Looking at the genogram that you've created thus far, how many marriages have ended in separation or divorce? Does the family talk openly about divorce, or is that a topic you

as a family skirt around? How do you feel about divorce? Can you describe the hurt that you've felt, or have seen and heard in the lives of other people who have been directly affected by divorce?

6. Can you identify any instances where a member of your family employs, or has employed, cutoff as a response to family conflict? Between parents and children, is there any evidence of fusion in the larger family or in any of the nuclear family units on your genogram?

7. Now that you have thought about marriage and your own response to conflict, and your family's response to conflict, it is time to speak with family members to get their views on these same issues. Here are some questions to get you started:

- How did your family talk about marriage?
- Was it expected that everyone in the family would get married?
- Are there any divorces in your family?
- How was divorce talked about—or not talked about?
- Did you ever see your parents or other married adults in the family argue? If so, what were those arguments about? How did their arguing make you feel? If not, how do you think they handled conflict?
- What were the expectations of how to handle strong emotions in your family?
- What happened when someone broke these "rules"?
- How were conflicts resolved?
- Were there any conflicts that didn't get resolved? How did family members handle that?

8. After you speak with your family, presumably you will have a lot more information about marriage and conflict in your family system. To indicate the emotional aspect of

the relationships in your family, use the symbols described in Appendix B under "Relationship dynamics symbols" and "Emotional relationship symbols." Although you should be aware of all the relationship dynamics and emotional connections between all family members in the genogram, within and between generations, for the purposes of the present exercise, zero in on yourself and the people you are most directly related to: (1) your parents (biological or step-parents), (2) your grandparents, (3) your sibling(s), and (4) your co-parent. In each of these relationships, indicate the relational dynamics and emotional connections within and between generations. To do so, first indicate how spouses/co-parents get along, and second, indicate how parents and children get along, (1) between your grandparents and your parents, and (2) between your parents and you.

When you finish this step, your genogram should represent not only the members of your family (e.g., names, birth, marriage, and death dates) by generation but also the interrelationships and emotional dynamics of your relationships with your parents, grandparents, sibling(s), and co-parent, and the co-parent relationships in each generation. If you step back from all the details and look over the big picture of your genogram, what patterns emerge? Does the genogram help you see these relationships from a new perspective, or help you understand things about how your family functions that you did not see or understand before? Which of these patterns do you want to embrace, which do you want to modify, and which do you want to change completely in your own life, in your relationship with your co-parent, and as a parent?

Figure 11: Genogram Step 4: Interpersonal and emotional relationships

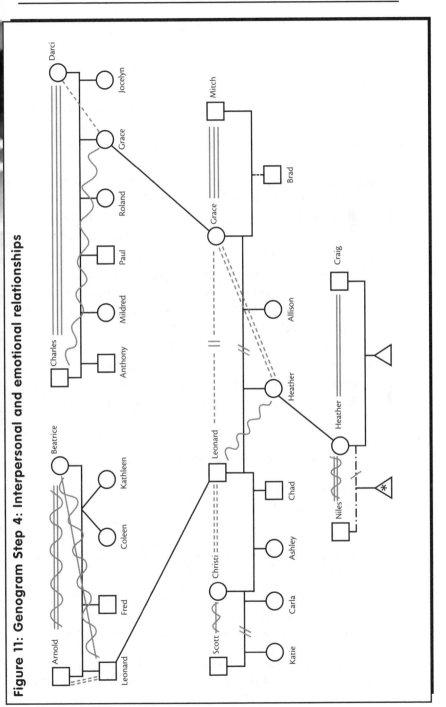

✚ Chapter Insights ✚

1. Your view of marriage is shaped by what you learned by observing and experiencing your parents' relationship. Gaining a realistic view of your parents' marriage, as an adult rather than as a child, can enable you to develop more reasonable set of expectations about your co-parent and your own marriage.

2. Relationships, especially marriage, involve conflict. Your marriage can survive hard times by approaching conflict with forgiveness and trust in your common commitment to one another. How you handle conflict will shape your family's future perhaps more than any other single factor in your life.

3. The presence of a third person (i.e., a child) changes the relational ground on which you stand from twosome (dyad) to threesome (triad). You may respond to conflict by means of fusion, cutoff, or any combination of these. What matters most is to develop habits of fighting fair.

4. Beware the "Four Horsemen of the Apocalypse": criticism, contempt, defensiveness, and stonewalling. The greatest remedy for healing a hurting relationship is God's grace.

✚ Resources ✚

Augsburger, David. *Caring Enough to Confront*. Ventura, CA: Regal, 1980.

———. *Caring Enough to Forgive*. Ventura, CA: Regal, 1981.

———. *The New Freedom of Forgiveness*. Chicago: Moody, 2000.

———. *Sustaining Love*. Ventura, CA: Regal, 1989.

Augsburger is one of the gurus of FST. His uniquely user-friendly approach to helping couples and individuals sort through the messages of their family system will not only give you a better understanding of FST, it will help you make real, workable shifts in your relationships with your family, your co-parent, and just about everyone else in your life.

Balswick, Jack O., and Judith K. Balswick. *The Family: A Christian Perspective on the Contemporary Home*. Grand Rapids, MI: Baker, 1989.

As a team, the Balswicks bring their backgrounds in sociology (Jack) and marriage and family therapy (Judy) together in this powerhouse of a book. If you only pick one resource on this list to have on your shelf, it should be this one. Their approach goes far beyond the theories of family life and actually guides you into new ways of thinking about what you want your marriage and your family to look like. Their advice is timeless.

Bilezikian, Gilbert. *Beyond Sex Roles*. Grand Rapids, MI: Baker, 1985.

If you or your co-parent find yourselves struggling with what the Bible says about the roles of men and women, Bilezikian's careful, theologically solid work will help you take a fresh look at these issues.

Gottman, John. *The Seven Principles for Making Marriage Work: A Practical Guide from the Country's Foremost Relationship Expert*. New York: Three Rivers, 2000.

———. *Why Marriages Succeed or Fail: And How You Can Make Yours Last*. New York: Simon & Schuster, 1995.

If you think you know what it takes to build a strong relationship, Gottman's work will surprise you. If you have no idea how to build a strong relationship, Gottman's work will inspire you. In both books, Gottman debunks much of what you might have heard or read about marriage and clues you in to the ways real couples wade through the muck and mystery of lasting love.

She's Having a Baby. Directed by John Hughes. Hollywood, CA: Paramount Pictures, 1988.

Sure, it's a John Hughes movie from the 1980s, but there's not a Molly Ringwald in sight. In fact, this very un-Hughes-like movie explores a new marriage and all its attendant adjustments. As you can guess from the title, it also follows this couple through their transition from two to three.

The Story of Us. Directed by Rob Reiner. Beverly Hills, CA: Castle Rock Entertainment, 1999.

Most movies romanticize marriage to the point where you leave the theater wondering how you got stuck in such a lousy, boring relationship. Here, then, is a glimpse of a much more realistic relationship, complete with a history of romance, hurt, memories, children, and regret. Few movies have captured what it feels like to be married better than this one.

Wallerstein, Judith, and Sandra Blakeslee. *The Good Marriage*. New York: Houghton Mifflin, 1995.

This groundbreaking book is based on the authors' study of fifty couples who identified themselves as having "good" marriages. Wallerstein and Blakeslee present what might be the most intimate look at someone else's marriage you might ever find. If you've sometimes wondered what the proverbial Joneses are up to, here's your answer.

Chapter 4

Your Family, Your Future

What we are teaches the child far more than what we say, so we must be what we want our children to become.

—Joseph Chilton Pearce

Becoming a parent will bring more changes to your life than you can imagine. One of the most surprising changes is how being a parent causes you to understand your family of origin. You will begin to look at your self and your family in totally new ways—some good, some not so good. As you adjust your life to make room for your child, you may find a deeper appreciation for the sacrifices your parents made for you. Or, as you hold your small, vulnerable child, you may feel a sense of resentment at the lack of love and care you experienced. When you make mistakes—and you will—you may develop a newfound respect for your parents' efforts to do their best for you. This can be a confusing shift. You may have thought you had your parents perfectly pegged. In your mind they were great or they were terrible; they were incompetent or they were perfect. When you become a parent, these labels may change. Consider yourself warned.

The journey into parenthood is an opportunity for you to forge new connections with the people who raised you. Many new parents find themselves turning to their own moms and dads for the first time in years. You may begin to think of your family of origin as a source of advice. You might call on them for wisdom and support. Maybe you grew up in the kind of family you wouldn't wish on your worst enemy. If so, you may have a hard time believing you would ever come to see your family as a source of parenting help. Fair enough. But consider all you've discovered about yourself and your family of origin over the last few sessions of *Shaping Your Family's Future*. You've seen that even the most troubled families have something to teach us about who we are. Even at their worst, they have a lot to do with what we believe and the kind of families we want to build.

 Talk It Over

As you begin this session, it's helpful to take an honest look at the way you were parented. This requires some emotional work on your part. Do your best to set aside your assumptions about your family. Instead, approach these questions with a sense of curiosity and compassion.

- What are some ways your parents expressed love and care for you? How do you feel about these expresssions of love now that you're older? Were they sufficient? How might your Enneagram relational pattern be connected to your feeling about your parents' expressions of love? What could your parents have done better to show their love?

- How does what you've learned from your genogram change the way you think about your parents? Do you believe they had the tools needed to parent you the way you wish you had been parented?

- What family parenting patterns do you see when you look back to how your grandparents raised your parents? What patterns do you want to hold onto? What patterns do you want to get rid of?

✖ Reaching Back ✖

A huge challenge in this type of work is to keep from using this as an opportunity to dump on your family. As you look over your genogram and ask these sometimes difficult questions of yourself and your family, you may be tempted to fix blame. You may be tempted to fault your parents, your grandparents, and other family members for problems in your life. Anyone whom you believe failed to be the kind of parents or people they should have been is a potential target of blame. The previous chapters were intended to help you see your family with new eyes. This exploration of the way you were parented will be just as helpful as you move forward into your life as a parent.

Your family system has a tremendous impact on nearly every aspect of your life as an adult. It can be easy to brush off the importance of dealing with the issues you've been exploring so far. This is particularly true when these issues are very painful or personal. Most of us are willing to put up with our own quirks as long as they don't really get in the way. But if you are to become a healthy, effective parent, these "quirks" are not something you can simply ignore.

Jared is a guy with an admitted anger problem. He grew up in a family where anger was freely expressed. His mother yelled a lot. His father yelled a lot more. His older brother also yelled a lot. When Jared was a young child, he assumed this was the norm. As he grew older and spent time with his friends' families, he began to see that yelling wasn't all that normal. Other moms and dads seemed to talk more than yell.

One incident in particular stood out for him. One fall, when Jared was about ten, he and his best buddy, Jeff, were playing around in Jeff's backyard. Jeff pulled out a book of matches. The two boys decided to set fire to some leaves just to see how fast they would burn. Naturally, the dry leaves caught fire quickly. Before they knew it, Jared and Jeff had started a fire. Not knowing what to do, the boys ran into the house and tried to act casual. They didn't want Jeff's mom to suspect what they had done. A neighbor saw the fire. He called the fire department, and the blaze was put out without much damage.

The boys watched from the living room window as Jeff's mom talked with the firefighters. They could tell from the look on her face that she knew what they'd done. She came into the house and called for the boys. Jared felt his heart race. He expected the kind of all-out shouting match he was used to at home. Instead, Jeff's mom calmly and firmly explained that she was very unhappy about what they'd done. In her quiet, clear way, Jeff's mom let the boys know they had done something very wrong. And just as calmly, she told Jeff he was grounded for a month and had to go without his allowance for two months to pay for the damage.

For Jared, this incident was less about fire safety than about anger. He was struck by the way Jeff's mom handled the situation. She left no doubt she was angry without ever raising her voice. He had never seen anyone do that before, and he never forgot it.

But in Jared's own family, the pattern of shouting continued. By the time he left for college, he had fallen into a habit of expressing his anger in the same way.

Even as Jared met and married Colleen, he knew his angry outbursts were hurtful. Colleen pleaded with him to find a different way to deal with his intense feelings. But Jared put off getting counseling or finding other kinds of help. He felt like his yelling was something he and Colleen would be able to work through. He didn't think it was the big deal she made it out to be.

After their first child was born, Jared and Colleen realized that Jared's yelling was a bigger problem than either of them had imagined. One night, the baby woke up crying several times. Colleen did her best to calm the baby. Jared tried to control his frustration over another night of interrupted sleep. But after being woken up for the third time, Jared lost it. He shouted at Colleen. He swore at her and the baby until both Colleen and the child were inconsolable. Jared angrily stormed out of the bedroom. He felt ashamed that he was turning out so much like his parents.

The next morning, Jared knew he had to do something about his anger problem. He remembered Jeff's mom and knew that was the way he wanted to deal with his children. He wanted to break the family pattern. He wanted to express his anger in ways that would help his family, not hurt them.

For Jared, parenthood became the invitation to change. He needed a different way to treat other people and a different way to think about himself. Parenthood motivated him to address these inherited patterns of behavior. Family Systems Theory (FST) calls this passing on of thought and action "multigenerational transmission." Basically this means that every generation of a family is shaped by the patterns of the generation before. These patterns may shift only slightly with each new generation. Small changes come as each adult in the family works to become his or her own person in the family of origin. They also shift as new people marry into the family system. (Each person brings his or her own "dances.") Sometimes this passing down is intentional. Parents teach their children how to behave around their elders or how to make Grandma's chili, for example.

Still, few families pay much attention to the emotional reactions and behaviors they pass on to the next generation. Parenthood brings out our most noble intentions. We want to be heroes to our children. We want their respect, their admiration, and their love. We genuinely want to be better parents than the people who raised us—just think of the mental list of "I'll never . . ." or "When I have kids . . ." promises you've made to yourself.

In the weeks and months before your child arrives, you may find yourself imagining the kind of parent you'll be. Maybe you see yourself as the cool neighborhood mom who loves having kids running through the house. Or you may dream of being the great dad who takes his kids fishing in secret water holes. Or perhaps you hope to be the calm patient parent who is always there with a hug, a word of advice, and a listening ear. You may very well turn out to be that kind of parent most of the time. You will find, however, that parenting tends to highlight your weaknesses. Along with your love, you'll show your children your impatience, your temper, and your selfishness. In revealing your shortcomings, though, you also become more authentic to your children. And it's just this mix of heroic intentions, intense love, and imperfection that pushes us to be people who create families we're proud of.

As you have seen in the previous sessions, inherited messages can be hard to uncover. They can be even more difficult to undo. In fact, it's impossible to rid yourself completely of these family patterns. They will probably always serve as your default mode. It's likely they'll show up when you're tired, stressed, or upset. But you can learn to sort through the messages you've received from your family. When you do, you'll find yourself on your way to being the kind of parent you want to be.

Parenthood offers you the chance to hold onto those patterns you cherish and to let go of those you don't. By connecting with your family of origin in new ways, you'll create healthier patterns for your children to inherit. This doesn't mean you have to move next door to your parents, grandparents, or in-laws. It simply means that you can make genuine attempts to form new kinds of relationships with them. As long as you become aware of your family's dance steps, and your role in them, you can pick which behaviors and attitudes to keep and which to discard.

Naomi grew up the only girl in a family of boys. She got along with her brothers. But she always felt a bit like an outsider in her family. Most of their family life revolved around the boys and their "boyish" activities. In an unconscious way, Naomi felt ashamed of being a girl. She felt like being a girl somehow made her less important than her brothers. Even Naomi's mother seemed to enjoy the hectic pace of keeping up with the boys more than spending quiet time with Naomi. It wasn't that Naomi didn't feel loved by the other people in her family. She just didn't know how to connect with them in a meaningful way because she was a girl.

As an adult, Naomi moved with her husband to another state. She stayed in touch with her family through e-mail and regular visits home. Curiously, she found that she didn't miss them all that much. But when Naomi became pregnant, she was surprised at how much she missed her family. She found herself longing to share this amazing experience with them. She wanted them to see her belly grow and her life changing.

> When Naomi's baby boy arrived, Naomi's mother came to stay for a week. Naomi's mother walked with the baby when he was fussy at night. She helped Naomi figure out how to wrap the baby in a warm blanket. She knew how to wash his hair without getting shampoo in his eyes, and other little mom "tricks" she'd picked up as the mother of four. The two shared tears as Naomi's mother recalled Naomi's birth. When Naomi's mother left to return home, Naomi realized they had experienced the kind of relationship she had longed for as a young girl. The shared experience of motherhood renewed a bond Naomi hadn't known was there.

When you become a parent, you'll discover that this new role can actually serve as a bridge between you and your family of origin. Grandparents tend to love their grandkids almost as much as parents do. This love will serve as a common passion that can give you a starting point for a new kind of relationship. You may find yourself turning to the adults in your family for all kinds of advice or support. Once you become a parent, your family may start seeing and treating you more like an adult. They may ask your opinion and take your decisions more seriously. Even stories about your childhood will take on new significance once you have a child of your own. Your child will become a person in whom you see glimpses of yourself. These connection points may come naturally, or they may take some effort. What's important is that you allow yourself to be open to the experience. Embrace the ways in which your new life as a parent can help you form a new relationship as someone's adult child.

For some, the idea of attempting a more meaningful connection with their family of origin might feel unwise. You may come from a family where it would be harmful—emotionally, spiritually, or physically—to you or your child to spend time with some family members. If that's the case, talk with your pastor or a therapist about other pathways to healing old wounds while avoiding further trauma. The whole purpose of creating new connections is to help you build a healthy family life for you and your children. In your journey to wholeness you have to remember that any changes you make have a ripple effect in your family of origin. The goal is not to reopen painful issues you've worked hard to overcome.

Dealing with your parenting heritage will be an essential step in becoming the kind of parent you want to be. In many ways parenting is where we are most closely tied to our past. It is one of the only areas in your life where most of us have just one primary example—our parents. (This applies even if you were raised by people other than biological parents. The people who raised you are your example of what parenting looks like.)

So, parenting is a part of your adult life where your family system has had a huge impact. But like Jared in the earlier example, you can overcome the negatives of your past by thinking beyond your assumptions about parenthood. You can begin to heal by replacing these automatic assumptions and reactions with a clear, intentional vision for the family that you are creating.

✚ The Purpose of Parenting ✚

Most discussions about parenting and family life assume that your main goal is just to survive the particular stage your child is in—infancy, the toddler years, adolescence, and so on. So the advice is geared toward the behavior and issues associated with children in that stage. Frankly, you'd have plenty to think about even if that was all that parenting involved. But shaping a family is a much richer experience than most parenting books lead you to believe. It is a sacred charge to be entrusted with the life of another human being. Think of the impact Gabriel's announcement must have had on Mary (Luke 1:26–38). It's a miracle to be given the priviledge of watching a child become the person she was created to be. A profound mystery lies in the heart of parenting, one that points us to the mysterious love of God.

The Bible doesn't say much specifically about how to be a good parent. The Bible has plenty, however, to say about how to live in this world—the book of Proverbs, perhaps, most obviously. It is filled with messages about how to treat others and how to live a life that brings about God's kingdom here on earth. All of that is what makes parenting matter. It isn't the way your children behave when they're at Grandma's that makes you a good parent. Rather, it's the values you instill in them. It's the love you show them and the love they in turn give to others. It does not come down to keeping certain rules, or doing things a specific way (Ephesians 6).

We have a tendency to look to the Bible for specific advice about every issue. We hope to find a verse or passage that will guide our decisions and tell us how to live. But the Bible is not meant to be that kind of advice book. Instead, it offers advice for some parenting and family issues and provides general principles for living in healthy relationships. But, more importantly, the Bible is the story of God's desire to live in a close and loving relationship with humankind, a story filled with accounts of how God shows intimacy and expresses love in ways that can heal and save us, despite the fact that we repeatedly turn our backs on God's free gifts of love, grace, and forgiveness. It's a story that continues on in our lives today. So when we look to the Bible for guidance, we need to be willing to look at the whole story, rather than pluck a few guidelines that match our notion of how to parent.

It's helpful to look at a passage that is intended to clarify God's desires for the nation of Israel.

> Hear, O Israel. . . . Love the Lord your God with all your heart and with all your soul and with all your strength. These commandments that I give you today are to be on your hearts. Impress them on your children. Talk about them when you sit at home and when you walk along the road, when you lie down and when you get up. Tie them as symbols on your hands and bind them on your foreheads. Write them on the doorframes of your houses and on your gates. (Deuteronomy 6:5–9)

Often this passage is used to tell us *how* to parent. A more careful reading makes it clear that it's really about *why* parenting matters. The subject of this passage is what is traditionally called the *Shema*. The *Shema* is the belief in one and only one God, and the response to this God is to love the Lord with our whole being. The point of this passage is that part of living as God's people is to instill a love for God in the next generation. "Love the Lord your God with all your heart and with all your soul and with all your strength." This is the legacy we are commanded to pass on to our children.

This is where the real power of parenting comes into play. It's an awesome responsibility to give a child a sense of being loved by the Creator. It's a terrific accomplishment to communicate a sense of being a spark of the divine light of God. Clearly, that doesn't happen by accident. It happens through careful, thoughtful, intentional parenting and through practicing how best to show God our love. And it happens by parenting with a concrete goal of creating a healthy family life. Only then will our children become responsible, caring adults who will in turn make their world more like the kingdom of God.

So how do you do this? The truth is, no one can answer that question better than you. You and your co-parent will be the primary people who know your children intimately enough to know what motivates them. Only you will know what scares them. Only you will know what concerns them and what excites them. You will be the only ones who will sense the subtle ways your children differ from one another and from every other child in the world. And so it will be you and your co-parent who have to figure out the "how" behind your own parenting. The responsibility of parenting, then, comes down to you shaping your child's future.

Still, answering this question of how you create a healthy family becomes much easier when you also know why you are parenting. That means having a clear guiding principle that shapes your parenting decisions. This goal goes deeper than hoping your child will be successful or have lots of friends. It requires thinking about the kind of human being you want to send out into the world. And it requires contemplating the kind of family life you'll need to nurture that kind of human being. It will mean talking about and living out the core values and beliefs you want to instill in your child. Most of all, it will mean recognizing that great families are never an accident. They are the result of intentional effort on the part of the parents grounded in the grace of God.

One model of family life that can be a helpful guide as you think about your parenting goals is Olson's Circumplex Model. Social scientist David H. Olson developed this model to help therapists assess the ways in which families function. Olson proposes three measures of family health: *cohesion, flexibility,* and *communication.* The most successful families find a balance within each of these three areas. While this might sound complicated, it's worth investigating. This model can help you and your co-parent develop a clearer vision of the kind of family you would like to create.

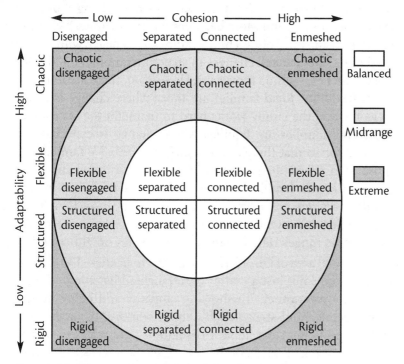

Figure 14: Circumplex model of family systems

Since Olson starts with cohesion, we will, too. *Cohesion* refers to the emotional bond family members have with one another. Families tend to fall into one of four levels of cohesion. *Disengaged* families are families where members are emotionally isolated and detached from one another. *Separated* families are those in which family members interact more than they would in a disengaged family, but also maintain some emotional separation. *Connected* families are families whose members share a close bond while maintaining their independence. Finally, *enmeshed* families are those in which family members are so tightly bonded they find it difficult to act independently of one another. The most successful and functional families tend to hit the levels in the middle. More often than not they find ways to function separately while staying connected with one another.

The second area to consider is *flexibility*. This measure is a reflection of how a family deals with change—changes in roles (Dad loses his job, and Mom becomes the breadwinner), changes in relationships (a young child becomes a teenager with a new level of independence), changes in structure (another child joins the family or Grandma moves in). Here again, there are four levels of flexibility. *Rigid* families are those where change is rarely welcome and the family works hard to maintain the status quo. *Structured* families are families where change is expected but planned for so that there are few surprises. *Flexible* families are those who adjust their expectations based on the changes life brings. *Chaotic* families exist where change is the norm and family members are always somewhat uncertain of their roles and relationships. Once again, the goal is to live in one of the two middle ranges rather than at the extremes on either end.

The final area of Olson's model is *communication*. Here, communication is not just a matter of talking and listening. It's also respecting each other. It's showing empathy and being honest about feelings and struggles. It's about working through difficulties and being clear about expectations. He refers to this as the "facilitating" dimension because it's what makes movement possible within the other two areas.

This model gives you a way to describe your family of origin and start visualizing the kind of family you want to shape with your co-parent and child. It allows you to say: We want to be a family where we trust each other and feel safe with one another (a connected family). We want to be a family that can adapt to the inevitable changes life will bring (a flexible family). We want to be a family where everyone can express their ideas, hopes, dreams, frustrations, and struggles (a communicative family). This process can then lead you to consider how you will create that kind of family.

Your vision for your family will likely change a bit as your child grows up and adds his or her own dreams and gifts to the mix. Still, the dreams you have for your family today will be the dreams you'll return to time and time again. They will be the map that will help you chart your course along the mysterious, magnificent journey of parenting.

Tom and Carolyn had been married for five years when their second child, Aaron, was born. Aaron's older sister, Camille, had been an easy baby. She slept well, ate well, and hit all of her developmental milestones pretty much right on time. But when Aaron hit the six-month mark, he had yet to roll over, coo, or show much in the way of interaction. He seemed to avoid eye contact and didn't respond to voices the way Camille had. Concerned, Tom and Carolyn talked with their pediatrician. He suggested Aaron may have something called Pervasive Developmental Disorder (PDD). Tom and Carolyn were devastated. They read up on PDD and learned that as Aaron got older, he might always lack interest in physical contact and have little desire for social interaction with other children.

This picture of Aaron's future changed everything for Tom and Carolyn. They began to see their family life through the lens of Aaron's disability. Would he have friends? Would he be able to attend a regular school? Would he ever get married and have children of his own? Would he be able to hold down a job? How would Camille deal with her brother? Would she bond with him if he was unable to bond with her? Would her needs start to get overlooked as Aaron's grew?

The vision Tom and Carolyn had for their family took a big hit with this diagnosis. As the initial shock of Aaron's disability wore off, Tom and Carolyn began to map out a new plan for their family. They would work to hold onto their core values of connection and intimacy with one another. And they would also expand their vision to include other families who were dealing with disorders like Aaron's. As a family, Tom, Carolyn, Camille, and Aaron started a support group for other PDD families. They found that this group allowed them to feel "normal" again. It gave them the support they needed to stay connected with each other. Other parents helped Tom and Carolyn find the words to speak with Camille about her brother's illness, and Camille made several friends who didn't think her brother was weird.

Aaron's diagnosis caused a major shift in this family's journey, yet their ability to be flexible made all the difference. They were able to talk about their concerns and to commit to staying close to each other no matter what.

Once you create a vision of parenting, hold onto it rather loosely. Parenting is not an "if/then" proposition. You can do everything right and things can still go wrong. Don't let that discourage you. There will be an abundance of happy surprises as well! But remember: parenting is not a job or a role. It's a relationship that will grow and change in unpredictable ways. Not only will expectations change as your children grow, but you will change as well. In ten years, you will not be the same parent, nor the same person, you are now. So be prepared to revisit your goals and dreams as you and your family move through life together.

Talk It Over

Work with your co-parent to come up with a vision for your growing family. Start by thinking about your family of origin and the pieces of your past that you want to carry into the future.

- Where does your family of origin fall on Olson's Circumplex Model's spectrum in terms of its cohesion, flexibility, and communication?

- Where on this same spectrum would you like to see the family you are creating?

- Think of at least three ways you and your co-parent can create a connected, flexible, communicative family.

- Review your genogram to identify patterns that you might have to change to reach your goals.

✚ Real Parenthood ✚

Parenthood, like marriage, is often overly romanticized in Western culture. Rarely do you see images of unhappy families in the movies or on television. Those you do see have seemingly obvious problems (think *Super Nanny* or *Mommy Dearest*) with seemingly obvious solutions. But most parents find some of their parenting hopes dashed pretty quickly. This can happen as early as when a delivery doesn't pan out the way you'd hoped. It can happen when your adopted child has a difficult time adjusting to your family. It can happen when that "instant" bond you hoped to feel for your child is slow in coming.

Before we have children, most of us have high hopes for our parenting abilities. We see ourselves as loving, patient, firm, and understanding. But one look at your family of origin and it's obvious that parenthood, like every human relationship, is incredibly complex and filled with pitfalls. That's why your parenting philosophy needs to extend beyond whether or not you'll spank your kids or how old they should be before they can begin dating. You'll want to build a parenting philosophy that will stand up to the reality of nurturing little human beings into adulthood. To do this, you'll need to look at how you view authority. You'll need to examine your beliefs about the part parents should play in the lives of their children. You'll also need to become aware of how you view the very idea of childhood.

Few of us stop to think about exactly how we view childhood. Not surprisingly, this is another area where the messages passed down from your family of origin have shaped your ideas. Understanding how you think about children is essential to figuring out the way you will parent your children. It will influence the way you talk to them, play with them, and discipline them. It will even influence the way you show your love to them. And all of that will, in turn, shape their sense of themselves. Your views will help form their ideas of God, of family, and of culture.

Tamika's parents divorced when she was eight years old. She didn't see much of her father after the divorce—just a few weekends during the year. As she grew, Tamika and her mother came to be very close. Tamika's dad didn't show much interest in her, and Tamika's mother knew this could have a terrible impact on Tamika's sense of who she is. So Tamika's mom made a concentrated effort to show Tamika that she was worth loving. She often talked about Tamika's character. She made it a point to notice when Tamika was kind to a friend or helpful around the house. She often asked Tamika's opinion on family decisions, like where they should go on vacation or what kind of pet to get. At the same time, she was careful not to turn Tamika into her confidant or buddy. She believed Tamika needed her mother to be in charge, to know she was safe in the care of her mother.

Growing up, Tamika didn't think much about her mother's parenting style. Even as a young adult, she wasn't aware of how intentional her mother had been in developing Tamika's sense of herself. But when Tamika became a mother herself, she began to recognize the choices her mother had made in an effort to help Tamika deal with her parents' divorce. As Tamika's own daughter started to walk and talk and become more independent, Tamika found herself facing the same kind of choices. When her daughter got frustrated trying to get herself dressed, Tamika resisted the urge to take over and instead praised her daughter's efforts and helped her tackle the task one step at a time. Because of her mother's example, Tamika knew that it was her job as a parent to show her daughter that she was a capable, valuable person, even at the tender age of three.

As you think back on your family of origin, you may have a hard time describing how your family helped shape your view of children. It can be helpful to think in terms of metaphors or word pictures. These can create a clearer sense of the relationship between the adults and the children in your family of origin. Each of the following metaphors represents one of what psychologists think of as four basic parenting styles.

These metaphors are based on the combination of control and support evident in each one. Imagine that you can measure the amount of control parents try to apply on a scale from low to high. Now do the same for the amount of support parents try to offer. Every parent falls somewhere on each of these two scales.

Support		
	High	Low
	Authoritative	Authoritarian
High		
Control		
	Permissive	Neglectful
Low		

Figure 15: Styles of socioemotional parenting

In the case of the Drill Sergeant, for example, there is high control, but low support. The Softy is just the opposite: low control, high support. Naturally, there are different levels within these metaphors and most families will demonstrate a range of parenting styles over time. Still, it's likely that one metaphor prevails in every family:

The Drill Sergeant (*Authoritarian Parenting*): Using the metaphor of a drill sergeant, the parent's role is to "train" the child. This is accomplished through clear expectations, firm discipline, and unquestioned authority. The child is to follow orders, stay in line, and experience the consequences of any disobedience or failure. The drill sergeant can certainly be a loving parent. However, the primary goal is to maintain control and order in the family system. Children in this metaphor are judged by their willingness to do as they are told without arguing or failing. A "good" child is the one who complies; a "bad" child is the one who resists.

This style of parenting might seem like a sure-fire way to develop good behavior in children. It fails, however, to instill self-direction or independence. One study reported that children raised in authoritarian families do well in school and have fewer behavior problems than other children have. However, they also have been found to have lower self-esteem, poorer social skills, and higher levels of depression than their peers do. This is mostly due to the perfection that authoritarian parenting demands of a child. This strips away a child's sense of self-worth. It makes it hard for a child to feel loved for who he is rather than for what he does.

The Autopilot (*Neglectful Parenting*): Parents in this metaphor tend to be emotionally and/or physically neglectful. It is important to recognize that this neglect is not necessarily intentional. Autopilot parents may have no idea how to talk to their children. They may feel at a loss as to how to establish family rules. They may be unsure of how to discipline their children. Or, they may just not have much interest in the daily work of rearing children. Their energy and interest may go instead to their work or their friends or their hobbies. Children are encouraged to be self-reliant. They are expected to ask for what they need, rather than having their parents recognize those needs and address them.

This style of parenting can often lead to something therapists call the "parentification" of children. Basically, this is exactly what it sounds like: Parentified children take on the role of the parent. This happens either because the parent refuses to take that role seriously or because the child senses the parent isn't up to the task. Parentification can happen, for example, in the child of an alcoholic who helps get his younger siblings ready for school when his mother is too hung over to do so. Or the child of a single parent who is her parents' sole confidant and emotional support system can slip into this role. Parentification is possible whenever parents are unable or unwilling to put the needs of their child ahead of their own.

The Softy (*Permissive Parenting*): These parents tend to respond *to* their children, rather than set up expectations and consequences *for* their children. Softies tend to be extremely lenient. They have few requirements of their children. The equation in their mind is "less rules mean more love," and "more rules mean less love." These parents often forgo corrective discipline or conflict because they don't want their children to experience shame or guilt. The child is seen as either a fragile, delicate creature who shouldn't experience the harsh realities of life, or as someone to be feared and appeased. Children in this view are typically allowed to make their own rules, so they experience few helpful boundaries.

There is a certain irony to this child-centered style of parenting. Parents who practice permissive parenting are usually motivated by the desire to make their children happy. But the lack of boundaries and expectations actually creates anxiety and insecurity in children. Permissive parents tend to be anxious parents. They tend to be overly focused on the needs of the child. These parents create a cycle where their anxiety about the child's happiness causes the child to be unhappy. This in turn causes the parents to work harder to make the child happy, and so on. In other words, the parents project their concerns onto their children, thereby creating the very thing they are worried about creating.

The Gardener (*Authoritative Parenting*): In this metaphor, parents respond to the individual needs of their children. They provide a stable, safe environment in which the children can grow. They see themselves as in charge, but understand that each "plant" in their care has its unique needs. They work to respond appropriately to those needs. Children are seen as individuals who thrive on a careful, personalized mix of discipline, nurture, and freedom.

Studies show that children raised by authoritative parents are also more socially skilled than are children raised under the other styles. Most of them do better in school as well. Authoritative parents allow children to experience success and failure under a safety net of love and care. Because it is based on a careful balance of control and support, authoritative parenting helps children mature and gain independence gradually and appropriately.

Obviously, the goal for you as co-parents is to find a balance of control and support. This will help you live out the dreams you have for your family. Finding that balance is one of the biggest challenges of parenting. You may worry that you will make horrible mistakes that will scar your children for life. But remember that parenting is a journey. You can and should make refinements along the way. Take stock regularly of what's working and what isn't. As the Circumplex Model discussed at the beginning of this chapter points out, flexibility is crucial to a healthy family life. Parents who remain willing to rethink their approach to rearing children are more likely to be parents who raise high-functioning kids.

The ability to recognize what needs adjusting is as much a skill as an instinct. There are people for whom understanding the needs of their children is as natural as breathing. But others find they are constantly challenged by the ever-changing demands of parenting. Children, after all, are complex human beings—they are no easier to figure out than the rest of us! But there are two basic tools you can use to see how you're doing: behavior and boundaries.

 Talk It Over

Consider the way children were treated in your immediate family and your extended family.

- How did this parenting style impact you as a child? How does it impact you as an adult?

- Take a look at Figure 11 above. Where would you place your parents on this diagram? Where would you like to see yourself as a parent? In what situations would you feel the need to exert more control over your child than usual? How about less control? More support? Less support?

Behavior

As your child grows, you will find that her behavior is the most obvious gauge of how she is maturing physically, emotionally, and spiritually. Behavior is an external sign of internal development. This means that your child's behavior is a reflection of what's going on inside her. For example, when a child consistently throws tantrums in public places, the tantrums are only the surface symptom. Naturally, the tantrums must be dealt with through timely responses and appropriate consequences. But smart parents try to figure out the cause of this behavior. Is the child easily overwhelmed by crowds or the intense stimulation of the mall, church, or grocery store? Is the child getting enough sleep? Are the parents' expectations for the child (e.g., to sit still for an hour of worship) reasonable for the child's age?

Behavior is your clue to your child's needs. Children have limited emotional language. Their feelings often come out through their behavior, rather than their words. Sometimes this acting out is on purpose. Just as often, it's done unintentionally. Consider that when you feel run down, you get grumpy. When you're stressed at work, you probably don't feel much like talking to your co-parent. Children are much the same. A child who seems to dawdle when getting dressed for school may be feeling some perfectly natural separation anxiety. A teenager who sulks in his room every night after dinner may be having a difficult time dealing with the changes in his mood and body. He may simply need quiet time. A child who can't sit still in church may feel bored and confused by the rituals and songs going on around her.

Your child's behavior is a good indicator of how you are functioning as a family as well. If your control/support balance is out of whack, you can count on your child's behavior to let you know. Children often act as a thermostat for the emotional temperature of their surroundings. If there is stress floating through the house, the kids will feel it unconsciously and respond with behaviors meant to release the tension they feel. Again, these behaviors are not necessarily intentional. Regardless, it's your job to help your child process these feelings. You can help by providing her with the words to name her feelings. It will serve the whole family well if you give her permission to feel and express her emotions appropriately. This is support in action.

This connection between behavior and your child's emotional life is not a reason to back off of consistent discipline. Discipline means to train and guide not just behavior but your child's character. The best discipline is the kind that sticks with this true meaning. The Bible says, "Train a child in the way he should go, and when he is old he will not turn from it" (Proverbs 22:6). Discipline, then, is the way in which parents help their children become the adults they will be one day. Taking a long-term view of discipline allows you to expand your "bag of tricks." Effective discipline is not defined by the desire to punish negative behavior. It is shaping positive behavior in an effort to nurture your child's character formation. This is where you'll need to find a healthy level of control. Exert too little and children won't learn how to function appropriately as adults. Exert too much and children won't have the tools they'll need to make good choices on their own.

Consider the way God "parents" us. God parents with love, grace, forgiveness, and an understanding of who we are and what we need as unique individuals. So when your child melts down in the grocery store, try to think beyond the moment. Consider what your child needs—security, attention, a nap— and act accordingly.

Boundaries

The idea of boundaries is familiar if we think of a map or a fence, but it might be quite foreign to you in the realm of internal, emotional, or relational space. This may be particularly true if you grew up in the kind of family without good boundaries. Really, the concept of boundaries is pretty straightforward. It's the idea that every person needs a combination of independence and relationships in which their independence is respected.

Like property boundaries, personal boundaries help you define what is yours and what is available for other people. This includes your time, your energy, your emotional investment, and so on. The hard part is figuring out where to draw those boundaries. This can be tricky when it comes to your children. Children are by definition needy. They need food and shelter and clothes and medical attention. They need time and attention and energy and love. They need to be taught, watched, studied, and understood. So it's not easy to determine when and how to say no to their needs in an effort to meet your own.

In her book *Connecting with Our Children*, psychiatrist Roberta Gilbert offers parents two lists to help develop appropriate boundaries with children. Look over these suggestions from her list carefully. Think first about your family of origin. Then consider the family you are creating with your co-parent. Later you'll have a chance to discuss these ideas with your co-parent.

Ten Ways to Invade Your Child's Boundaries

1. Tell her what to do when you know she knows what to do.
2. Dress her when you know she can dress herself.
3. Check his room needlessly.
4. Take too much of a part in school activities.
5. Talk about him to his brothers/sisters.
6. Talk about her to her friends.
7. Worry.
8. Hover.
9. Make a bigger deal than necessary out of hairstyles and clothing.
10. Think about her more than you think about yourself or your relationship with your co-parent (Gilbert 1999, 141).

Ten Ways to Allow Your Child to Invade Your Boundaries

1. Answer all questions.
2. Ignore kicking or screaming or other unacceptable behavior that is affecting other people.
3. Need to always be liked by your kids.
4. Need to always rescue.
5. Allow children's "divide and conquer" technique to cause trouble in your relationship with your co-parent.
6. Feel you must buy/supply anything asked for whether or not you can afford it.
7. Defer to children on making major family decisions.
8. Leave your bedroom door unlocked even though you want time alone.
9. Worry about your kids when you are out for the evening.
10. Lose sleep because of unresolved curfew behavior (Gilbert 1999, 142).

Boundaries might not seem very important right now and that's okay. You are about to enter into the stage of parenting where there really are no boundaries, at least not right away. The needs of a new baby or an adopted child *must* come first. This will be true for as long as it takes for that child to gain some autonomy. But you'll be surprised how quickly that happens. As soon as a baby is able to fall asleep on his own, he has developed a bit of autonomy. As soon as your child starts reaching for her bottle or trying to wiggle out of your arms, she is showing you she is ready to try doing things for herself.

The most basic life journey is the move from dependence to independence. Fortunately, it begins almost immediately after birth. There's a saying that as soon as a child is born she begins the process of leaving you. Your goal as a parent is to help your child mature into an independent, responsible adult. It's part of that job to develop the boundaries that help that happen.

Rose and Miguel are the parents of a preschool-age son, Joseph, and an infant daughter, Juanita. Rose had been an elementary school teacher before her children were born, but she and Miguel decided she would stay home once they became parents. She was excited to use her teaching skills to help her own children learn and develop. When she had just one child, she and her son spent much of their day together. They would read, do art projects, and go for nature walks in the neighborhood.

When Juanita was born, it became more difficult for Rose to spend long stretches of time with Joseph. Once Juanita was a bit older and had a regular nap schedule, Rose found herself conflicted about time. She would try to use the time to play with Joseph. But she also knew that the baby's naptime was her time—a chance to grab a shower, do some laundry, or clean up the breakfast dishes. Her "free time" became the time to do all the other household chores that were tough to do with a baby in hand. Still, Rose believed the housework could wait. After all, these precious days with her children would be over too soon.

When Rose was a child, her own mother Isabella was kind and loving in her own way. But Rose didn't feel like her mother was very nurturing. Isabella often let Rose play by herself while she did the housework or made dinner or talked on the phone. She was not the kind of person to sit on the floor and play with her children. Rose vowed to be a more involved parent.

After Miguel and Rose started to take Joseph to preschool, Rose wanted to help out in her son's preschool class. Having Juanita made it tough for her to get as involved as she'd hoped to be. When the class went on field trips, Joseph begged Rose to chaperone, but she just couldn't find anyone to care for Juanita. This made Rose feel like she was failing her son.

Rose also began to feel guilty over the lack of one-on-one time she had with Juanita. When Joseph was born, it was just the two of them for most of the day. Rose loved the long hours she could spend just gazing at him. But she felt like she barely had time to look at Juanita, much less gaze at her. Rose agonized over how to balance her time so that she would meet the emotional needs of both of her children.

Aside from Joseph and Juanita, Rose also missed the personal time she could steal when Joseph was a baby. She longed for the days when she had time to read a book or even a magazine article. Now that she had two children, she felt like she had to give them every spare moment.

In her desire to make each moment count for her kids, Rose also lost sight of her relationship with Miguel. She was committed to raising Joseph and Juanita in an environment filled with stimulation. She envisioned their childhoods filled with life lessons and precious memories. But her dreams were bumping into the reality of the dirty details of life with young children. This, of course, meant lots of messes, lots of demands, and very little time. And the stress of not taking time to nurture herself or her marriage took its toll on everyone.

Rose's story is a common one, especially for parents who want to throw themselves completely into parenthood. Saying *no* to a child's request for playtime so that you can wash the dishes can feel terrible. Parents might fear they are sending kids the message that housework is more important than they are. But in truth, it's okay for children to have to occupy themselves sometimes. It's okay for them to play alone and figure out what to do with their time. Trying to meet all of their needs all of the time can burn parents out. It also makes kids overly dependent on their parents.

Setting boundaries doesn't make you neglectful. It doesn't make you selfish. In many ways, maintaining healthy boundaries between you and your child is the most *un*selfish thing you can do. It's okay to let your children make mistakes, solve their own problems, and experience failure, even when it makes you look bad. Healthy boundaries are those that allow everyone in the family to be themselves and to meet their basic needs.

The presence of healthy boundaries is also a sign that your control/support levels are in balance. When boundaries are missing, the balance goes with them. You may find yourself feeling tapped out because of the demands of parenting. If so, the odds are good that you are trying to have too much control over your children or are offering them more support than they need. You may be trying so hard to meet their needs that you are ignoring your own. And when parents are stressed out, everyone suffers.

The kind of parent you will be depends a great deal on your ability to make intentional choices for your family. Every significant decision you make as a parent needs to be rooted in a purpose. Being a good parent doesn't mean you have to be perfect. It doesn't mean you have know what you're doing all of the time or even always be consistent. There's a huge learning curve here! Instead, positive parenting is about paying attention. It's about thinking about what your children need and being willing to try again when things don't work the way you'd hoped. It's about keeping the big picture in mind in the midst of a thousand little decisions. Most of all, parenting is about shaping your family's future in a way that nurtures the tender lives God has placed in your care.

Talk It Over

Talk with your co-parent about behavior and boundaries.

- What behaviors were forbidden in your family of origin? What behaviors were encouraged?

- What behaviors will you refuse to tolerate as a parent?

- What kind of discipline will you use to encourage appropriate behavior?

- What character traits do you hope to help your children develop?

- What kind of guidance will your children need to build these character traits?

- Were there some suggestions on the boundary lists you disagree with or were surprised by? How might that action cross a person's boundaries?

✜ Homework ✜

Your genogram work for this session involves looking over your family history for parenting patterns. This step is designed to help you gain a clear understanding of the kind of parenting modeled in your family, as well as factors that shape your own parenting, such as multigenerational transmission, cohesion, flexibility, communication, and boundaries. Keeping in mind the concepts discussed in this chapter, speak with members of your family of origin to learn more about the parenting assumptions, expectations, and ideals that are part of your family heritage.

Genogram—Step 5

1. Before you knew you were going to be a parent, what ideals did you hold about parenting? Can you trace any of those

ideals to people you know (e.g., your own parents or grand-parents, parents of friends)? Do you still hold the same ideals as you enter parenthood? When you think of the role of a mother and a father, what kinds of responsibilities fall under each of these roles?

2. What were your expectations of your parents during your childhood and adolescence? Did they measure up? If not, where did they fail?

3. What expectations did your parents have of you and your siblings? How did you know what those expectations were? How did they discipline you if you didn't do what they expected? Did they establish boundaries for you?

4. How did your family communicate with one another: verbally, in writing, with facial expressions and body language? Were you just expected to know what someone else was thinking or feeling? Did you feel like you were truly heard when you tried to communicate in your family system?

5. With your own ideas about parenting fresh in mind, speak with your parents and siblings about their memories and perceptions of how the family operated. Here are some questions for your family members to help you get started:

   - How did the women in your family talk about motherhood? Fatherhood?

   - How did the men in your family talk about fatherhood? Motherhood?

   - How were children expected to behave within the immediate family? What about in the extended family (e.g., with grandparents, etc.)?

   - How would you describe your family's level of cohesion or closeness?

   - What rituals or traditions were important in your family? How did these get passed on to each generation? For instance, did you grow up in a family that took the same vacation every year—same place, same time, same people, and so on?

- What were some of the life-changing or relationship-changing events your family experienced? How did they handle the changes?
- How did your family talk about change? Was it welcomed? Expected? Feared? Prepared for?
- Which of the parenting metaphors describe your parents? Your grandparents?
- How did your family members express their connections to each other? How did they express their independence from each other?

6. Look over the responses you get to these questions. What do they tell you about the view of parenting and family life in your family? What did you learn about the origins of your parents' ideas about family? What patterns do you see in your family? Is there a common expectation about behavior? Are there similar messages about discipline or the place of children in the family? On a separate piece of paper, put the label "Parenting in My Family," and write down any surprises or insights you gained about your family. Attach this sheet to the back of your genogram project.

7. Many factors determine how effective communication is within the family. And any two people may employ different styles and techniques of communication at various times. If you try to represent all the lines of communication and how people are communicating in your family, your genogram will get way too messy. While you should keep notes about these details for your own reference, we will opt for a simpler way to show communication. On your genogram, draw two-way arrows between you and your parents, between your parents and their parents, and between the spouses or co-parents on your genogram. In the middle of each arrow, insert a (+) for effective communication or a (-) for ineffective communication. This may not be detailed or exact, but it gives you a quick reference point in looking at family communication. When you finish, count the number of pluses and minuses on the genogram. What does this reflect about your family's mode of communication?

Figure 12: Genogram Step 5: Parenting, communication, and conflict

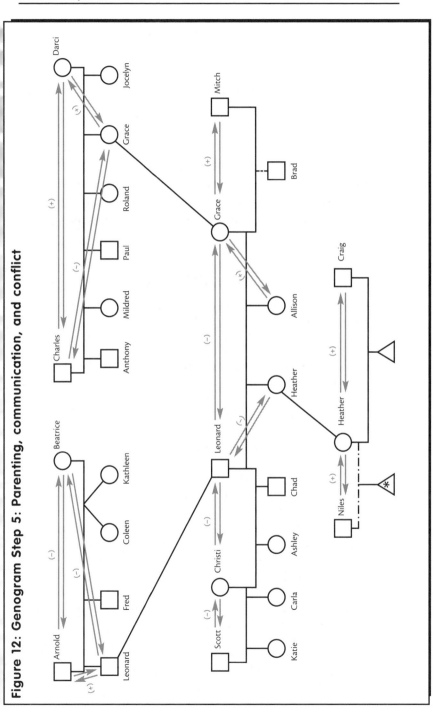

✚ Chapter Insights ✚

1. You will serve your children well by becoming aware of patterns that seem to show up in multiple generations of your family, and choosing to embrace the healthy patterns and putting an end to unhealthy ones.

2. The goal for co-parents is to find a balance of control and support, which defines what type of parenting you prefer: authoritarian, neglectful, permissive, authoritative.

3. Observing behavior and setting boundaries will help both you and your child find the balance of a healthy family.

✚ Resources ✚

Clapp, Rodney. *Families at the Crossroads: Beyond Traditional & Modern Options.* Downers Grove, IL: InterVarsity, 1993.

Clapp brings a theologian's perspective to family life, offering fresh insight into what the Bible says—and doesn't say—about family life. Clapp takes a hard look at the ways in which cultural expectations have infiltrated the evangelical understanding of family and helps parents rethink our ideas about what family looks like.

Cloud, Henry, and John Townsend. *Boundaries with Kids.* Grand Rapids, MI: Zondervan, 2001.

Cloud and Townsend are the masters of boundaries. This extraordinarily practical book is indispensable for parents who want help setting loving limits, finding balance, and minimizing the stress of parenting—in other words, everyone.

Covey, Steven. *The Seven Habits of Highly Effective People.* Revised edition. New York: Free Press, 2004.

Covey's advice for business leaders has multiple applications for families. Covey's emphasis on setting priorities and living by your values will inspire you to see parenting as more than changing diapers and driving the minivan.

Gilbert, Roberta. *Connecting with Our Children: Guiding Principles for Parents in a Troubled World.* New York: Wiley, 1999.

Gilbert's work applies Bowen's Family Systems Theory to everyday parenting, making this the perfect resource for parents who want to have a deeper understanding of how to make the most of all you've learned through *Shaping Your Family's Future.* Filled with practical ideas, real-life examples, and thorough analysis, Gilbert's book will serve as an excellent resource that you'll return to again and again.

Goldberg, Myla. *The Bee Season*. New York: Anchor, 2001.
This is the story of a family in crisis: a crisis of identity, of change, of subtle shifts in roles. It's a fascinating examination of how delicate the family system can be and how easily it can be undone by the simple actions of its members.

The Joy Luck Club. Directed by Wayne Wang. Hollywood, CA: Hollywood Pictures, 1993.
This film, based on Amy Tan's 1989 novel of the same name, tells the story of four first-generation Chinese American women struggling to form their own identities in the shadows of their immigrant mothers. It's a beautiful example of parental hopes and the ways in which they can both motivate and cripple children. Whether you read the book or see the movie, you will gain a new understanding of the power of parenting.

Chapter 5

Enlarging the Circle— Your Family Gets Bigger

*A healthy social life is found only when in the mirror of each soul
the whole community finds its reflection, and when in the whole
community the virtue of each one is living.*

—Rudolf Steiner

In the summer of 2004, film director M. Night Shyamalan
released a movie called *The Village*. The movie tells the story
of what, at first glance, appears to be an isolated nineteenth-
century community in the woods of Pennsylvania. The people
of the community live in a tense relationship with the unseen
creatures who live just beyond the edges of their town. There is
an age-old agreement that these creatures will not enter the village as long as the villagers do not enter the woods.

But it is soon revealed that the village actually exists in
present-day America. Having grown up in the "outside" world,
the village elders were disillusioned with the violence and apathy
they saw around them, so they formed a new society where there
would be no crime, no killing, and no danger. The "creatures"
were a myth (and, as it turns out, so was the eighteenth-century

setting) that they invented to keep their children from discovering the truth and venturing outside of the village.

The movie itself received poor reviews. Still, the story illustrates the way many adults feel when they become parents. Suddenly the outside world begins to threaten everything you want for your precious child. Every stranger becomes a predator waiting to prey on your child. Every place other than home becomes a deathtrap or a place where you could lose your child. The world is suddenly filled with sharp objects, steep staircases, and unknown dangers. The instinct to protect our children from physical, emotional, and spiritual harm is compelling. It can lead us to pull away from all the "negative" influences of the culture. It makes us want to see only those things that reinforce the vision we have for our children. Some parents may, as in *The Village*, build a wall around their children to prevent them from coming into contact with that threatening world.

Shaping Your Family's Future discusses the relation between family and community because the family is no more isolated from the society in which it lives than you as parents are isolated from your family and its influences on your parenting. Sooner or later, every family decides how it will relate to the surrounding culture. This is rarely one big decision but rather a series of little choices made every day. Families decide how much emphasis they will give to work and money. They determine what kind of media and technology they will include in their daily lives. They choose how they will interact with their neighbors, their church, and the broader community. These decisions are all based on the view a family has of society. In some families, the culture is something to be feared or blamed. In others, the culture is something to be embraced. Still other families give little thought to pop culture at all.

As with all of the other topics in *Shaping Your Family's Future*, the way you and your co-parent relate to the culture around you will be largely influenced by your families of origin. Even your ideas about what "culture" means will differ depending on your background. Amish communities view secular culture with great suspicion. What view of culture were you taught as a child? For the sake of this session, we will use the word culture as a way of talking about the society in which we live. You will also come across the word "community" in this session. We will use that term to describe the people and places with whom you have regular interactions—your neighborhood, your town, your church, your workplace. As you will see, the influence of your community and the value you place on that community will also have a tremendous impact on the way you view culture. The term culture is used here in the sense of "the body of customary beliefs, social forms, and material traits constituting a distinct complex of tradition of a racial, religious, or social group" (*Webster's Third New International Dictionary, Unabridged*).

Hannah grew up in a deeply religious home. Her father was a pastor, and Hannah and her siblings knew his word was the law. Hannah's parents had determined that there were several aspects of the "secular" world that were not suitable for their children. They did their best to protect their children from these influences. The children attended a private Christian K–12 school. They couldn't watch television without their parents being there. They could listen only to Christian music and were not allowed to go to movies at all. Growing up, Hannah wanted to please her parents. She trusted that they knew what was best for her. She never felt the need to rebel against these restrictions.

When Hannah reached college age, she spent her summers working at a Bible camp she had attended as a child. One evening, several staff members decided to head into town to see a movie. Not knowing Hannah's family rule, they asked Hannah to join them. Hannah had never been to a movie, but thought it would be okay. The movie was rated PG and her parents would never know she'd seen it. Besides, she reasoned, she was an adult and capable of making her own choices.

As the group drove into the theater parking lot, Hannah grew nervous. What if my parents happen to call the camp and someone tells them I'm at a movie? Suddenly, Hannah broke out in a cold sweat and began to feel physically ill. She felt a rising sense of panic and nausea. By the time Hannah and her friends reached the door of the theater, Hannah knew there was no way she could enjoy the movie. Even so, Hannah sat and watched the movie with one of her friends. After the movie was over, she wrestled with her sense of shame over disobeying her parents.

When Hannah became a parent, she began to understand her parents' restrictions in a deeper way. She loved her baby so much and wanted nothing more than to protect her from harm. She knew this was the impulse behind her parent's strict expectations. Yet Hannah also remembered how it felt to be paralyzed by the fear of making a bad decision about something as simple as watching a movie. She and her husband decided they would do their best to resist reacting hastily to mainstream culture and instead try to make thoughtful and informed choices about the way they relate to the culture around them. They also resolved to teach their daughter how to make good choices for herself.

For Hannah's parents, religion was the guiding force in determining how they related to the popular culture. Quite simply, Christianity and culture were mutually exclusive, even contradictory. Their approach may seem unusual to you, but their view of culture makes perfect sense in their worldview. As the gospel song puts it, "This world's not my home, I'm just a-passin' through." The bottom line is that our thoughts on culture are actually products of a circular pattern of influence. Our view of the predominant culture around us is shaped by the culture itself.

It can be helpful to think of society as a super-sized family system. Every society has its own set of expectations, norms, and values. As in the personal family system, the expectations of a cultural family system are often unspoken. These messages play a huge role in the way people in that system think. The values of the system become the values of the people in the system.

For instance, those of us who live in the United States have a very different understanding of the role of the individual in relation to the community than someone living in a traditional African tribe. American culture is based on the idea that every person is responsible for his or her own well-being. We value the "self-made" millionaire and the single mother who "pulls herself up by her bootstraps." On the whole, we place great emphasis on self-reliance. We value the freedom to make our own choices. We strive for personal success and work to protect our individual rights. We enjoy the rewards of our successes and the penalties of our failure. But tribal societies emphasize helping the community. They emphasize working for the common good. They value contributing to the whole rather than concentrating on an individual's role. A child growing up in a tribal culture likely never thinks about her rights or her individual needs. In fact, she probably never thinks of herself as an individual apart from the community at all. She knows her "self" only as a part of something much bigger than herself. Her identity comes from her place in the tribe.

Of course none of us belong to just one culture. We are also influenced by smaller spheres of the bigger mixture of cultures where we live. We identify with our religion, our local values, our political beliefs, and our ethnic ties. These communities can have just as much influence on our worldview as the broader culture. So it's important to figure out what impact these communities had on your family of origin.

Sorting through these messages is, as you know, essential when thinking about the ways you want to deal with cultural issues as a parent. You'll want to consider how they will affect your child and your whole family. This process will help you determine which messages you agree with and which you don't. It will help you decide if you will see the influence of the world as something to be embraced or something to be feared. This in turn will shape the way you parent and the future of your family.

A person's view of the culture informs his or her engagement with that culture. This is true not just in the broad sense but also in many particular ways. Robert Putnam, author of *Bowling Alone*, notes,

> All things being equal, people who trust their fellow citizens volunteer more often, contribute more to charity, participate more often

in politics and community organizations, serve more readily on juries, give blood more frequently, comply more fully with their tax obligations, are more tolerant of minority views, and display many other forms of civic virtue. . . . Experimental psychologists have shown that people who believe that others are honest are themselves less likely to lie, cheat, or steal and are more likely to respect the rights of others. (Putnam 2000, 136–37)

What's interesting about this is not only what it tells us about people but also the assumption that lies behind it. This view suggests that we can have an "us" and "them" mentality toward the society in which we live. In truth, it's impossible to separate ourselves from the culture in which we live just like we are part of the family into which we are born. Our culture trickles into all aspects of our lives. In looking at your family of origin and the way you have been shaped by your family system, you've seen that we are products of our familial environment. This part of Family Systems Theory (FST) is called Societal Emotional Process. It describes how the culture as a whole impacts individual family systems and the people within those family systems. Each system is part of and influences every other system.

Consider the ways that you and your co-parent will relate to the culture in which you live. Recall what you've learned about family systems so far. Just as you want to have an interdependent relationship with your family of origin, you will want to establish a perspective on your culture that allows engaged participation, sound criticism, and healthy boundaries. You want a place in the culture where you are emotionally connected yet able to make decisions based on your family's needs and values, rather than some cultural script.

Talk It Over

Spend some time talking as a group about the ways your families related to the culture and the ways the culture influenced your family.

- How would you describe the relationship between your family and the broader culture: Suspicious? Blaming? Indifferent? Involved? Fearful? What gave you this impression?

- How do you believe you have been influenced by your family's view of society?

- What does your family focus on when it talks about the evils of the culture? What vehicles convey pop culture (e.g., TV, advertisements)?

✚ What Your Community Can Do for You ✚

Since your community is made up of the people and places you interact with most often, this is where your decisions about cultural interaction will play out. This is also where you can find clues about the way your family of origin thought about culture and community.

As you think through the questions above, keep in mind that the questions we ask ourselves about community are often quite different from those of our parents and grandparents. The ways we experience community have changed tremendously in the past fifty years. Author Joseph Myers explains it this way:

> In the 1940s and 1950s we were on the move. . . . The term "bedroom community" described the phenomenon of the separation of work and home. For the first time we lived closer to work than to family. . . . As we spent more time at the workbench than around the dining room table, our personal and intimate connections slowly changed. We experienced a pervasive disconnect with our traditional

family relationships and turned inward to find the answer. We searched for the significance that was once experienced through the family tree. . . . The self-help movement fed an individualistic consumer movement. We grew in our awareness of individual needs and wants. . . . Somewhere along the way we lost our extended families, and our public and social connections could not sustain the community conversation. (Myers 2003, 122–24)

It's not that previous generations were more community minded than we are. Rather, they didn't have to think about community as intentionally as we do. For most of our parents and grandparents, community just happened; it was a result of being near people. Your grandparents likely lived closer to their extended families than you do. They likely lived in much smaller towns than you do. They likely lived and worked in the same part of town. We, on the other hand, have to work at creating a sense of connection with other people. When we don't, we risk becoming isolated in ways our parents and grandparents never experienced.

The truth is that we need our communities. We are meant to be part of something bigger than ourselves. Our families are meant to be part of something bigger. The Bible often uses metaphors to help us understand the ways in which we are meant to live. It's not a coincidence that many of these metaphors deal with connectedness. For example, the apostle Paul tells us we are the body of Christ (1 Corinthians 12:12–27), individual parts that make up a unified whole. Jesus says he is the vine and we are the branches (John 15:5), another interdependent system. Even the image of a family comes into play when we are called the children of God (Hosea 1:10). Paul explains this need for connection this way: "God has combined the members of the body and has given greater honor to the parts that lacked it, so that there should be no division in the body, but that its parts should have equal concern for each other. If one part suffers, every part suffers with it; if one part is honored, every part rejoices with it" (1 Corinthians 12:24–26).

Ming and her husband, Chi, were high school sweethearts. They have been married for five years. Shortly after they got married, Ming was accepted to a prestigious graduate program in another state. Moving meant leaving behind both of their families, many friends, a church they loved, and Chi's job. But both Ming and Chi believed this was an opportunity they couldn't pass up.

Ming and Chi were both surprised by just how deeply they missed home. Ming called her mother nearly every day. She needed to check in and catch up on the daily events of her hometown. Chi began to feel the stress of getting adjusted to a new job and adapting to life in another city without his brothers and sisters to talk to. When they discovered that Ming was pregnant, Chi and Ming seriously considered returning to their hometown. They longed for the familiar faces of family and friends.

Instead, they decided to stick it out so Ming could finish her program. Still, Ming found that expecting a child made her miss her old life even more. She longed to share the experience of being pregnant with her mother and her best friends. Her classmates didn't pay much attention to her pregnancy. She had established few connections outside of school. When Ming was seven months pregnant, she and Chi started taking a childbirth class at a local church. After the first session, one of the other couples asked if anyone would like to grab coffee at a nearby café. Ming and Chi decided to go. They quickly found that the shared experience of becoming parents made it easy to connect with these new friends. Over the course of the class, Chi and Ming made a real connection with this couple. Together they all agreed to stay in touch once their babies arrived.

This initial connection led Chi and Ming to a church home. It led to more friendships. It even provided contacts that helped Chi find a better job. They began hosting a small home group of young people from their church. They met every other week with a group of ten people for dinner, conversation, and prayer. These connections spurred Chi and Ming to practice other kinds of hospitality. They began sharing their home with a single student who needed temporary housing. And they established an "open door" policy for their friends who often stop by just to hang out. They regularly invited neighbors over for dessert or Saturday morning for pancakes. These small acts of community involvement have been just as good for Chi and Ming as they have for those on the receiving end of their graciousness. Chi and Ming now feel like they have solid roots in their community. They have begun to think of themselves as "home."

Connecting with your community doesn't necessarily mean becoming a "joiner." You don't have to sign up for Bible studies and other kinds of clubs or groups. You can become connected through more casual relationships—hanging out with friends, hosting a neighborhood cookout, grabbing a movie with people from church. As evidenced in Chi and Ming's situation above, joining a specific group, such as a childbirth class, can easily lead to casual connections and vice versa.

As individuals and families move from place to place more frequently, they leave behind family and friends. Our mobility affects both the family and the community where we live; further, it forces us to rethink what family and community are.

> On the first day of elementary school, Danielle, whose family recently moved to town, is the new kid on the block and an outsider. She's far away from the extended family that she left behind where she used to live; so now Danielle has only Mom, Dad, little brother, Don, and their furry shih tzu, Aristotle. At school, she doesn't know anyone, nor do they know her—no friends, no gang, no social place to call her own. Her classmates won't become a community for her until she is welcomed into a group of friends, gets invited to birthday parties and sleepovers, wins a part in the class play, and begins to feel like this is her school. Then her newly formed community will provide some of the support she used to receive from her family.

Danielle's experience illustrates how family and community are changing. More importantly, her story brings home the point that families should not isolate themselves from the communities in which they live. When we see ourselves as belonging to a community, rather than as an outsider, our definition of family can expand to include more than just the people with whom we share DNA, a home, or a history. Where people care for one another, support each other, look out for each other, and create a safe place to be who they are, they form strong bonds with each other. Outside of the family, these bonds of friendship and community free us to live without fear of the society around us.

Talk It Over

- What institutions were your family members involved in: public schools, politics, the church, civic clubs, arts groups, parachurch organizations, and so on? What does this involvement tell you about what your family valued or didn't value in the surrounding culture?

- How did these community institutions influence your family? What messages of these communities did your family accept? What messages did they reject?

Talk with your co-parent about the ways in which you can expand your understanding of family to include your community.

- What kind of formal social activities are you involved in? Civic clubs, art lessons, political activism?

- What kind of informal social connections do you have?

- How much time do you spend on these activities? Do you wish you spent more time involved in these activities or less time?

- In what ways have these activities helped you feel more connected with your community?

- Thinking back to your Enneagram relational pattern from Chapter 2, consider the kinds of social activities that might be most meaningful to you—volunteering, leading a group, running for public office, etc. How can these activities address your basic desires?

- How do you see your family life coming together with your social life?

✠ What You Can Do for Your Community ✠

Connecting with your community can be a beautiful way of extending your sense of family. It can also have a tremendous impact on your children. Robert Putnam points out the following:

> A considerable body of research dating back at least fifty years has demonstrated that trust, networks, and norms of reciprocity (meaning a belief that helping other people will mean others will help you down the road) within a child's family, school, peer group, and larger community have wide-ranging effects on the child's opportunities and choices, and hence, on his behavior and development. Although the presence of social capital (that is, communities where people trust each other, join organizations, volunteer, and socialize) has been linked to various positive outcomes, particularly in education, most research has focused on the bad things that happen to kids who live and learn in areas where there is a deficit of social capital. The implication is clear: Social capital keeps bad things from happening to good kids. (Putnam 2000, 296)

And get this: Putnam says that states that score high on the Social Capital Index are the same states that score low on infant mortality rates, drop-out rates, teen suicides and homicides, teen pregnancies, and crimes committed by teenagers (Putnam 2000, 296). Naturally, many other factors are at work here—economics, education, and, of course, family systems—but it's safe to say that community matters to children, as well as to parents.

Developing intentional connections within your community has benefits that go far beyond helping you and your family develop a sense of belonging. As you strive to live an integrated life, community and family become so closely connected that it's hard to think of them as separate. In fact, the more involved you become in your community, the more you will understand that this involvement is a crucial part of your family's emotional, social, and spiritual formation.

However, the connection between family and community is not a one-way deal. Just as families need the community, the community needs families. Back in chapter 4, you spent some time thinking about the purpose of parenting. The idea was that parenting is essentially about nurturing children so they grow into healthy, responsible adults. That understanding of parenting is rooted in the idea that family life is an extension of society. We want our children to become adults who improve the world. Theologian Stanley Hauerwas writes, "The family is not just something we do because we are in the habit, nor is it something we do to fulfill a moral pupose. Rather marriage and the family . . . [become] a vocation for the upbuilding of a particular kind of community" (Hauerwas 1981, 174). This understanding of family life makes us want to instill a sense of communal responsibility and belonging in our children. We do this through the ways we choose to interact with the culture and the people around us.

Being aware of the community and turning our attention to what is happening there, as well as paying attention to what is happening in our family, makes us other-centered. With a focus on our neighbors' needs and the situations they face, we turn attention away from ourselves. And the good thing about being other-centered is that when we are, we keep our own problems in perspective. In doing so, we gain a more balanced view of our family.

What a family does with its time, energy, and money communicates the family's values to children. It tells children what their parents believe to be important and what they believe to be unnecessary. Author Tim Stafford talks about family culture and the way it shapes the character of the members of the family. He considers this concept different from family traditions.

> Family culture should not be confused with family traditions. Family traditions include practices like reading the Christmas story on Christmas Eve, watching the annual Big Game at Grandma's house or making Velvet Chocolate birthday cakes. Traditions make up part of family culture, but family culture is larger. It embraces everything we do, even (especially?) practices we follow without realizing we are doing anything peculiar. . . . Some families have lots of traditions, and some have very few. All families have lots of family culture. Family culture is simply the particular way you do things in your family—everything from how you celebrate the New Year to

how you make lunch. . . .Culture is habitual ways of life transmitting values into practical living. (Stafford 2004, 15–16, 19)

In many ways, Stafford is talking about family systems—the assumptions, messages, and practices that make each family unique.

Stafford's point is that the best way to instill values in our children is to create a family culture that is reflective of those values. Step 1 is to identify these values. Once you've done that, consider practices that will help you instill these values in your kids. Stafford offers these suggestions based on the Bible and God's desire for how we are to live.

1. *God first (Deuteronomy 6:5).* Honoring God comes before anything else.

2. *Concern for others (Galatians 5:14).* Jesus told us to love our neighbors as we love ourselves. That means constantly and scrupulously paying attention to their welfare.

3. *Hard work (Colossians 3:23).* Whatever we work at, we should do it wholeheartedly.

4. *Truthfulness (Ephesians 4:25).* Our words should be filled with truth and no words that undercut that truth.

5. *Generosity (Luke 6:30).* God wants an overflowing and openhanded love for others, especially in how we invest our possessions.

6. *Submission (Ephesians 5:21).* In many different settings—work, marriage, church, government—we fit into a larger scheme and submit to the leadership of someone else. Submission implies accepting our limited role in the world.

7. *Sexual fidelity (Ephesians 5:3).* Faithfulness to a marriage partner implies eliminating anything that interferes with our love for that partner. Single people express sexual faithfulness by living chaste lives.

8. *Family unity and love (Psalms 133:1).* The family is a core unit that demands respect, support, and love. So does the church, as God's family.

9. *Boundaries (Proverbs 4:23).* God has given each individual certain areas of responsibility that belong to him or her alone. First is his or her body. Next is his or her property. Jobs, family, and relationships may also be private. These areas of individual responsibility should be protected.

10. *Joy and thanksgiving (Philippians 4:4).* Celebration should be part of every day because we recognize all that God does for us.

11. *Rest (Hebrews 4:10).* We work within the limits of time and ability God has given us. After working, we need to stop for renewal.

12. *Care for creation (Genesis 1:28).* God made humans responsible to develop and care for all that God has created.

13. *Contentment (Colossians 3:15).* With whatever we have and whatever we are, in whatever place or position God has put us, we should learn to be at peace.

14. *Grace (Colossians 3:13).* We are meant to follow in the footsteps of God himself, offering forgiveness and grace to others even when it isn't deserved. (Stafford 2004, 24–26)

You may have noticed that all of these values have a relational element. They all involve the way we connect with other people. This is where this sense of the family being an extension of the community comes in. The values you choose for your family will seep out into your community. They become part of the larger system as your children play with friends, go to school, get jobs, head to college, and on and on. Family life is never confined within the walls of a house. It plays out in the everyday interactions we have with others. This includes our neighbors, friends, and extended family, even strangers. Your children will learn how to be involved citizens, loving spouses, and tender parents in the context of your family life. This is where they will learn how to be reliable coworkers and thoughtful friends. The values you choose and implement will become the touchstones of your children's character.

Once you've decided on the values that will be the core of your family life, you can begin to think about day-to-day family practices that support these values. For example, maybe hard work makes your list. To instill this value in your children, you might sign them up for piano lessons. Learning music demands patience, diligence, and practice. In short, it involves learning to work hard. Or you might have a family chore day where everyone pitches in to keep the house clean and functional. That practice calls for teamwork, persistence, and humility. These are also elements of being a good worker. The practice itself is less important than the values it teaches.

Tricia grew up in a family of artists. Her mother was a gifted musician. Her father was a sculptor and art teacher at the local community college. They didn't have a lot of money. Still, when Tricia thinks about her childhood, she pictures a house full of music, people, and laughter. Naturally, Tricia's parents got her involved in all kinds of artistic endeavors. She took dance classes. She had painting lessons. Although Tricia enjoyed these activities, she never really found a creative niche like her parents did. As she got older, it became clear to Tricia's parents that she had a gift for math and science. When she headed off to college with plans to be a doctor, they couldn't have been prouder.

There seemed to be tremendous differences between her parents' lives, which centered on the creative process, and Tricia's life, which revolved around science. Tricia found, however, that her parents' influence was a real asset in her medical career. As a doctor, Tricia was often more willing to try something out of the ordinary. She was more open to experimental treatments or non-Western medical options than many of her classmates. She had a deep understanding that music and art could be used as effective therapeutic tools. Tricia welcomed the input of other doctors. She believed that there was value in the process of healing, not just in the end result. Tricia was often complimented on her unique approach to medicine. She always says, "I think medicine is often more of an art than a science. Sometimes it involves a willingness to look at a problem from an unexpected perspective in order to find a solution." Clearly, her parents' emphasis on creativity was not lost on their daughter.

As you consider both the values and practices that will form your family culture, be aware that this whole process is about helping your child grow. Instead of getting stuck on rules and regulations about behavior, help your child become the person God created her to be.

This kind of focus on values and character formation makes family more than just a group of people who happen to live together. The family becomes part of the community. More importantly, it becomes part of the future and part of God's kingdom on earth. Children who learn that there is more to life than meeting their own needs grow into adults with a sense of purpose. What a great gift it is when we show our children that their lives matter!

And so we return to the community and its place in your family's life. We are people whose lives are woven into the fabric of our culture. The values we choose to live by will be played out in the communities in which we live. This interplay between your family and your community means that your children will come to see the world around them as one of God's gifts. They will experience community as the stage on which their God-given gifts and passions play out. In church, for instance, we have an obligation to use our gifts to build up the body—God gave us gifts for us to give them away. Understanding community as an extension of your family helps you find the support you need to thrive as a parent and as a person. Recognizing that we are created to live in relationship with other people—all of God's people—motivates us to seek the kind of life that allows us and our children to grow into the people God created us to be. Instead of holing up in the "village," you are now prepared to live in a way that is deeply connected with others. You're ready to be a family that recognizes that the world only gets better when we are active participants in its ongoing redemption. And that is family life at its best.

Talk It Over

Work with your co-parent to determine the values you want to emphasize in your family. Consider the values you inherited from your family. Contemplate the values of the society and communities where you live. Then, look over Tim Stafford's list and discuss the importance of each suggested value.

- Which values on the list above seem like "no brainers" to you? Which ones seem unnecessary?

- What values would you add to this list?

Now make a list of ten to fifteen values you want to focus on as a family. Don't worry about how you will do this yet, just talk about what matters most to you.

Look over the list of values you created. Now spend time brainstorming practices that will help you live out these values as a family. Start by thinking about some of the activities you were involved in as a child and the "life lessons" you learned. Then consider the activities you envision your children being involved in. For each of the values on your list, try to come up with two or three practices that would underscore those family values.

✚ Homework ✚

Your homework for this chapter will take far more than a week. In fact, it might take years to complete it. Now that you've worked through the ways that your family of origin impacted your views of faith, your self, marriage, family life, and the broader community, it's time for you to take all you've learned and launch yourself into the next stage of your life as a person and as a parent. The genogram that you are completing can be the springboard for ongoing growth.

In thinking of how your family relates to the larger community, a similar kind of project that you might consider completing is called an ecogram. Like a genogram, an ecogram looks at the relationships and factors that shape you and your behavior, both individually and as a family. However, the ecogram turns attention to social factors outside of the family that affect the family and the individuals in it. If you complete an ecogram, you will look into schools and extracurricular activities, churches and social organizations, as well as doctors, jobs, economic conditions, environmental disasters, and everything that influences your family's life. Even if you don't forge ahead with that project, your genogram will have laid the foundation for you to understand the potential impact that the larger world has on each family unit.

Genogram—Step 6

1. As you were growing up, to what degree did you feel your family was involved in the larger community: a lot, a little, or not at all? Describe the community that served as the social network for your family. What kinds of groups did your family contribute to or rely upon for help? How involved were you personally in social groups outside of your family? What social groups were most important in shaping you and which ones meant the most to you at the time?

2. How did your family view popular culture and its influence on you? Was the culture in which you lived just taken for granted? Was it something your family talked about, but accepted because it could not be changed? Or, did your family view culture as something not to be trusted, an enemy to fight against? Can you think of a story from your past that best illustrates what you remember about this?

3. In what concrete ways did culture shape your values as an individual and as a family? In what ways did you try to shape the values of the culture around you, if at all?

4. As you review what you've learned from doing the genogram, what concrete goals would you like to establish for yourself and the family that you and your co-parent are creating? What steps would you like to put in place to achieve

those goals, individually, as a parenting couple, and as a family? And how do you think the changes you plan to implement in your life will affect your children, siblings, parents, and larger family of origin?

5. On the genogram, next to each family unit, write the names of organizations or communities that played a significant part in that family's life. Then draw a circle around the list of names.

6. Once you see the community connections in graphic form, ask yourself whether you perceive any overlap or new insights into the influences from outside the family that shaped who you are today.

Reflections on the Genogram

The point of *Shaping Your Family's Future* is to equip you to be the best person, and therefore the best parent, you can be. A big part of your journey to wholeness is taking a close look at the people and events that led you to this place in your life. It's also about where you go from here. You cannot step into the future without a strong sense of how you have been shaped and how you want to shape your own children. You can't act on all you've discovered without a game plan. You should be ending this course with just such a plan in hand.

Your genogram can form the foundation of your future. Look back over all the questions you've asked, the answers you've been given, the patterns you've discovered. Then look ahead to the chapter that you are writing in this family history. Where will you follow the path blazed by your family? Where will you blaze your own path? When the time comes for your children to look back over their history, what will they see or say? What connections will they make? What will they add to this story? These are the questions that give parenting its purpose.

Your mission from here on out is to apply what you've learned. Start right now. If you have a strained relationship with your family of origin, now is the time to start to find a way to heal those old wounds. Reconnect on new terms. Forgive what

Figure 13: Genogram Step 6: Family and community

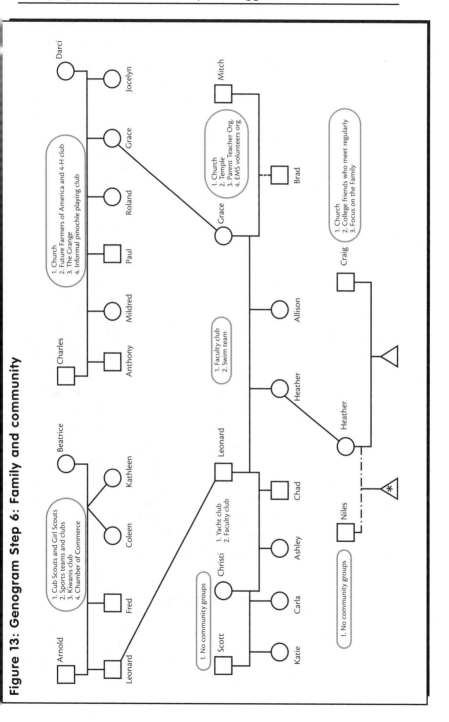

needs forgiving. Accept what can't be changed. Make the phone call. Have the conversation. Go home. Take the chance and trust that things can get better. If the work you've done here has made you appreciate your family even more, then tell them. Deepen the connections that are so important as you create a family of your own.

Most of all, this is the time to develop your support network. Enlist your family, your friends, the people in this *Shaping Your Family's Future* program, or a combination of all of those people. Parenting is not something we are meant to do alone. It truly does take a village for families to survive. Your village is made up of grandparents, aunts and uncles, neighbors, babysitters, teachers, and on and on. German theologian Dietrich Bonhoeffer, who was executed by the Nazis for participating in a plot to assassinate Hitler, said in his book *Life Together*, "Christian community is not an ideal we have to realize, but rather a reality created by God in Christ in which we may participate" (30). In other words, you are part of a community whether you try to be or not. This community of family and friends is God's gift to each of us.

If you take nothing else away from this course, you should take this: God loves you as you are. You and your family are part of the ongoing story of God. This story reaches back through the generations that came before you. It will continue until long after your children are grown and raising children of their own. The idea that we parent not only for our children but for the generations that will follow them is both noble and humbling. This notion of parenting can keep you from stumbling over the details of raising children. It can help you focus on the big picture, on the journey that you and your children will travel together.

✠ Chapter Insights ✠

1. Just as individuals are not islands, so also families function in and are influenced in various ways by larger communities; and you need communities as much as they need you.

2. Communities remind you that you and your family are part of and responsible to something much larger than your clan. The diversity and support of communities can enrich family life.
3. Your family can have a positive impact on your community as well. In the give-and-take of family life, you can model for the community a better way to relate to one another.
4. Seeing your family as part of a broader community involves you in making choices about the values and character you wish to form in your child. Whose values and what character traits do you want to reinforce or teach your child to avoid?

✢ Resources ✢

Bellah, Robert et al. *The Good Society*. New York: Vintage, 1992.

This book, a follow-up to *Habits of the Heart*, explores the civic institutions that define a society—schools, churches, governments, and so on. While it is a bit academic in tone, this book is an essential resource for understanding the connections between individuals, institutions, and the culture.

———. *Habits of the Heart*. New York: Perennial Library, 1986.

If you're not convinced we are creatures of our culture, this book will convince you. Through an extensive survey of Americans across the economic, religious, and political spectrum, the authors have created an overview of American life and the assumptions, values, and ideologies it promotes. Again, the book is a bit academic, but you won't find a better explanation of the ways we are shaped by the society we live in.

Bonhoeffer, Dietrich. *Life Together: A Discussion of Christian Fellowship*. Harper & Row, 1954. Originally published, 1938.

Hauerwas, Stanley. *A Community of Character*. South Bend, IN: University of Notre Dame Press, 1981.

Another dense theological book, Hauerwas emphasizes the role of character in Christian ethics and the ways in which our Christian communities can shape us into people of conviction and compassion. If you enjoy theology, philosophy, ethics, or just a good argument for faith, this book is a winner.

Myers, Joseph R. *The Search to Belong*. Grand Rapids, MI: Zondervan, 2003.

Myers explores the human need for connection and points to ways we can connect to our neighbors, our coworkers, and our families. A quick read, Myers's book is aimed at church leaders, but his ideas can easily be applied to family life.

Putnam, Robert D. *Bowling Alone: The Collapse and Revival of American Community*. New York: Simon & Schuster, 2000.

One more thick book that deserves reading, Putnam's study puts to rest the myth that adults today have no interest in community and civic life. On the contrary, Putnam show that adults today are as civic minded as previous generations. He makes a case for diving headfirst into community life for the good of ourselves, our children, and the culture itself.

Palmer, Parker. *The Company of Strangers: Christians and the Renewal of America's Public Life*. New York: Crossroad, 1981.

Palmer applies theories of public life to the religious experience, demonstrating the need for churches to become more than just places of worship, but places of real community and cultural involvement.

Stafford, Tim. *Never Mind the Joneses*. Downers Grove, IL: InterVarsity, 2004.

This book is the perfect resource for parents who want to create a meaningful family life. Filled with practical ideas, as well as solid theology, Stafford's book shows parents how to instill biblical values in their children through sports, music, family time, and community involvement.

Tortilla Soup. Directed by Maria Ripoll, Hollywood, CA: Samuel Goldwyn Films LLC, 2001.

The story of a Hispanic man and his three adult daughters hinges on the force of the cultural expectations at work in one family. As each of them deals with the ups and downs of life—dating, aging, working, relating—we see how their culture both encourages and gets in the way of their ability to make choices and move forward with their lives.

Afterword

By now you have come a long way from the start of your journey into *Shaping Your Family's Future*. This may be a good time to reflect on any new understandings or insights that you have gained. What have you learned about your self and how your family of origin has shaped you? Has your understanding of your parents' relationship or your perception of your siblings changed? Do you have any new insights into what you bring to your relationship with your co-parent? Have your thoughts about parenting changed in any way?

Some persons will have gained new insights into their families of origin. For some, what they've learned may have been unexpected and perhaps a bit unsettling.

Between the first session and now, this program asked you to invest a lot of time and effort in creating your own genogram.

However much energy you spent doing that, as you probably discovered, you could spend countless more hours revisiting the issues raised by that search for insights into the connections between who you are and how your family functions. As you review your genogram, you may want to put a star next to the three or four areas you wish to pursue in the months and years ahead. Hopefully, you have expanded your understanding of who you are, where you came from, and how you would like your new family to be in the days ahead. By the time your child is ready to become a parent, what sage advice will you be able to offer her or him, based on your genogram journey?

One of the unanticipated benefits of working through the *Shaping Your Family's Future* program in a group is the relationships you develop with your classmates. In addition to learning about your self and your co-parent, we hope that you have also gained insights from the experiences of others in your group. These group sessions have provided a unique opportunity to share your questions, struggles, and triumphs with other parents. From week to week, you got to listen to their perspectives on the same issues you struggle with, and hopefully they have contributed to your growth as an individual and as a parent. You have both learned from and had opportunity to share your viewpoints with others. Everyone in the group deserves a big thank you for the part they played in preparing one another for the challenges and opportunities of parenting. We hope that you have developed into an active support network for one another. Take advantage of this valuable network as you venture into this new stage of life.

Shaping Your Family's Future is designed to help you develop the resources you need to parent with your eyes, mind, and heart wide open. As you begin to understand the ways your family history shaped your identity and how that history affects you as a parent, you now have the chance to shape *your* family's future. Given the new perspective on parenting that you gained over the past six weeks, what intentional choices do you plan to make about the kind of person you want to be and the nature of family life that you want to have? Rather than blindly following the examples from your past, you can now move into parenting with the freedom either to embrace or to set aside family patterns. You should have a good start on moving toward a deeper, more meaningful connection with your past and your future, so you can become the best parent you can be. This course most likely has brought about several big changes in how you view God, your self, your marriage, your family, the church, and the community around you. Your sense of who you are may have changed as you discovered the importance of your role as a parent. Your relationship with your co-parent has changed as your focus shifts to your child. Your relationship with your family and friends has changed as you begin to see yourself as part of something far bigger than your own household. Your understanding of God also has changed as you have discovered the ways in which parenting brings out a sense of life purpose you may never have experienced before.

You have learned about faith formation. A family's view of spiritual issues enters every aspect of its collective experience. It informs the family's sense of purpose. It frames the parents' philosophy about children. It impacts the way the family fits into its community. It influences how families spend their money, the activities in which the kids are involved, and how they celebrate holidays. Whether God was the resident policeman, the parental hangover, the meek and mild caregiver, or the managing director, how your family of origin perceived and taught you to perceive God impacted your life dramatically. In turn you will impact the lives of your children as you teach them the role God plays in your life today.

You have learned about different relational patterns through the Enneagram. You charted your own Enneagram, as well as those of your family members in your family of origin. These various relational patterns affected the roles played by your family members and resulted in a unique family dance. With this knowledge you can now make an objective assessment of the messages you received about yourself from your family of origin, and you can understand your subjective view of the way you see yourself functioning in the world today. You now have a stronger grasp of the ways your self-concept has been shaped, and you can better understand yourself. You have the tools you need to be intentional about shaping your child's sense of self. In short, you are better equipped to make parenting decisions. Your choices are based on who you really are and what you really value, rather than on the roles and values you *think* you should have.

You have learned about the dynamics of marriage and how these dynamics shift when a child enters the picture and takes the original dual relationship you had with your spouse and transforms it into a triangle. You have seen that how you interact with your spouse affects how you will be as parents and that the behavior you exhibit will teach your child how to behave when she becomes an adult and starts a family of her own. Do you want your child's model of marriage to be based on dismissive or preoccupied behavior, or a secure, loving relationship that promotes healthy interactions? You have learned to build the kind of strong, stable friendship you need to have with your spouse to make the transition into parenthood. God created us to be in intimate, meaningful relationships, and marriage is a precious gift from God, one that is worth tending to and preserving.

You have applied this knowledge to your plans for the future of your family. What kind of parenting style would you like to develop, and how would you like your family members to interact with one another? Will you be the drill sergeant, the autopilot, the softy, or the gardener for your growing child? Do you want your family to be rigid and disengaged, or flexible and connected? You have learned about respecting your child's boundaries as an individual and, in turn, not allowing your child to cross your own boundaries as a parent. Through all of these complex decisions, you know that communication and balance are the keys to building a healthy family dynamic. It happens through careful, thoughtful, intentional parenting and through practicing how best to show God your love. And it happens by parenting with a concrete goal of creating a healthy family life. Only then will your child become a responsible, caring adult who will in turn make his world more like the kingdom of God.

You discussed the important relationship between family and community. The family is no more isolated from the society in which it lives than you as parents are isolated from your family of origin and its influences on your parenting. Every family decides how it will relate to the surrounding culture. The influence of your community and the value you place on that community will also have a tremendous impact on the way you view culture. No matter what that view is, though, community plays an important role in your child's life. As the values of your community affect your child, the values you choose for your family will seep out into your community as well. They become part of the larger system in the everyday interactions you have with others. Through your family's interaction with the community around you, your children will learn how to be involved citizens, loving spouses, and tender parents. The values you choose and implement will become the touchstones of your child's character, and your child's character will shape the future of our world.

Shaping Your Family's Future is only a starting point, though. Unless you do something with what you have learned, this book is no more than words on a page. You owe it to yourself, your co-parent, your child, and to the future of your family to put into practice what you gained from this program. It's your life; live it to the fullest with the gifts of God's grace and mercy.

Appendix A

A Family System at Work

Chad walks to his car after leaving his fourth-grade classroom at Washington Elementary. As he starts the engine, he notices a familiar churning in his stomach. He was fine while managing a room full of fidgeting ten-year-olds, but thinking about his wife, Rachel, and their infant son, Jason, at home makes him nearly break out in a cold sweat. Chad loves his family, but for reasons he can't quite name, the thought of walking into his home sends waves of panic over him.

Chad married Rachel, the love of his life, four years ago after a thirteen-month courtship filled with romance and roses. For Chad, marriage was a new experience, but Rachel came into it after a painful divorce from her first husband of two years. A few years had passed before Rachel met Chad through a mutual friend, and Rachel thought she had learned from her mistakes. From the first date, she was attracted to Chad's gentleness and easygoing nature. He couldn't have been more unlike her immature, hotheaded first husband.

Aside from Rachel's natural beauty, Chad admired her inner strength. He respected the way she had come through a difficult time and made a good life for herself. She seemed confident and strong. Three years into married life Chad and Rachel had their son.

Chad and Rachel knew about pregnancy and caring for infants from their birthing class. They read many books on the subject before Jason's arrival. What they didn't understand was how much stress and conflict they would experience after they brought Jason home from the hospital. Chad loved the elementary children with whom he worked, and Rachel had assumed he would be a natural father. Instead, he seemed nervous around the baby. He usually let Rachel soothe Jason when the baby was fussy or needed his diaper changed. At first, Rachel didn't mind when Chad deferred to her, and she was eager to prove her mothering skills. After a few months, however, she became increasingly frustrated. She felt that Chad just assumed she would do the bulk of the caregiving. The tension between them became more intense when Rachel's maternity leave ended and she went back to work full time.

During Rachel's pregnancy, she and Chad had discussed having Chad care for the baby during his summer break. But as the summer grew closer, Rachel became less sure that Chad was up for full-time parenthood. When she brought up the option of having her mother care for the baby a few days a week, Chad quickly agreed. This did not make Rachel feel better. Instead, she found herself resenting Chad for what she saw as abandoning his responsibility.

Before long, Rachel stopped asking for Chad's help with Jason altogether. She quietly assumed they were all better off if she just did most of the work. She knew that her mother would do a fine job caring for Jason. Still, she felt let down by Chad's apparent unwillingness to step up to the call of fatherhood.

Things weren't much better from Chad's perspective. Chad had been excited during Rachel's pregnancy. He loved to listen to the baby's heartbeat. He enjoyed seeing his son flip around on the ultrasound. Chad had always liked children and he, too, was sure he was going to love being a dad. But when Jason was born, Chad was bothered by how disconnected he felt. Who was this new little person living in his house? He didn't feel the rush of love Rachel seemed to experience. During the first several weeks, Jason seemed to cry more often than not. Chad couldn't figure out how to comfort him. He felt discouraged when Jason would cry in his arms and stop only when Rachel would take over. Chad did occasionally change Jason's diaper or rock him to sleep, but he felt like Rachel was always reminding him to use enough diaper wipes or insisting he wasn't holding Jason the right way. At bedtime, Rachel would hover, following Chad into the nursery and watching as he put Jason in his crib to make sure he did it properly. As the summer approached, Chad panicked at the thought of being home alone with Jason for hours on end with no relief. When Rachel suggested having her mother help out, Chad believed that was the best option.

Still, he felt like he'd let Rachel down. He felt like he was a failure as a father. He was discouraged and let Rachel take over most of Jason's care. Even on the days when he was home with Jason, Chad struggled. He just didn't know how to fill the day. He often ended up calling Rachel or her mother for help or advice.

✦ Behind the Scenes ✦

As you can see, things aren't going so well at Chad and Rachel's house. It's easy to play armchair quarterback for this family. We might assume that everything would improve if only Chad would take more responsibility or if Rachel would quit nitpicking. But solving relationship problems is never about quick fixes. The key is to figure out what's leading to the problems. Why is Chad is struggling with fatherhood? Why does Rachel feel the need to control the situation? Why does she resent Chad's disengagement.

Figuring out what's at the root of these struggles involves looking at the once-underlying issues that are working themselves to the surface now that Chad and Rachel are dealing with the pressures of parenthood. It involves looking at the assumptions, expectations, and understandings Rachel and Chad inherited from the family systems in which they grew up.

Rachel

Rachel, the oldest of three children, grew up in a fairly traditional family. Her father worked as an accountant. Her mother stayed home with the children. When Rachel was nine, her father died unexpectedly of a sudden heart attack. This forced her mother to go back to work. By default, Rachel took charge of her siblings. Rachel's mother was often critical of Rachel's performance as housekeeper. She would get angry if Rachel forgot to take clothes out of the dryer. She complained about dirty dishes left on the table. Rachel understood that it was hard for her mother to be a single parent. As a result, Rachel did her best to keep the peace at home and anticipate her mother's needs. At the same time, she started taking out her own anxiety on her younger brother and sister. She often yelled at them when they made a mess or didn't follow through on their chores.

Without consciously choosing to do so Rachel now acts much like her mother. She is determined to show others she can recover from difficult situations (like her divorce) and move forward. She is also prone to being a perfectionist, in part because it was often hard for her to please her demanding mother. As the oldest child, Rachel is used to being in control. She is accustomed to having others do things her way. Chad's laid-back nature was appealing to her at first. Now she simply believes he acts like a child. In her mind he gives up when things don't go his way. She wishes he could be more like her and her mother and take some responsibility in his life.

Chad

Chad is the younger of two children. His father is a well-respected doctor. His mother was a stay-at-home mom who devoted herself to the children. She baked cookies and played games with Chad and his sister. She served on the PTO and volunteered at Chad's school, while Chad's father was rarely home when the children were still awake. He left early and came home late. Chad felt that even when his father was home, he wasn't all that interested in spending time with his children. So while Chad was close to his mother he had a tenuous bond with his father.

Even as a teenager, Chad had a good relationship with his mom. When he was a junior in high school, he and two friends were arrested for shoplifting at a local convenience store. When Chad's parents were called, his father was unable to get away from work to come to the police station. Chad's mother was there right away. After talking with the arresting officer, she managed to get the charges against Chad dropped. Chad and his parents never talked about the incident again, but Chad knew that his mother had saved him from some serious consequences.

Chad has always had a hard time making decisions, in part because his father often seemed critical of Chad's choices. Chad played football, but his father would have preferred that he play basketball and rarely attended Chad's games. When Chad considered attending a public university, his father derided him for not aiming higher and applying to a more exclusive private school.

As the youngest child with an older sister, a doting mother, and an essentially absent father, Chad is used to having others take care of him. He is not incapable of taking care of himself, but when given the choice or faced with a stressful situation, he'd just as soon let others do the work. One of the things he loves most about Rachel is how responsible she is, how she takes care of all the little details of their life together. Still, it bothers him when she is critical of his ideas or ways of doing things. He wishes she would learn to relax and not take everything so seriously all the time.

✠ Family Systems Theory ✠

Chad and Rachel's relationship gives us a good illustration of the ways a person's family of origin influences their beliefs and behavior. We'll use their story to explain the basic concepts of Family Systems Theory (FST).

Triangles

Regardless of age, individual people come genetically prepro- grammed to think and act in certain ways. This applies to both someone's personality and social predispositions. These are influenced as well by factors such as birth order and patterns of family interaction. This mixed bag that we call "the self" does not live in isolation. Most of us live and work, go to school, and play with other people. We get involved in churches, syna- gogues, and civic organizations. We interact with other people.

Each time we connect with another person, we create a "dyad" or couple (not in the romantic sense, but in the "two- person relationship" sense). We all know from experience that two-person relationships can take a great deal of time and energy to maintain. And when problems arise, it can be hard for two people to cope with all of the emotional stress. So couples unconsciously pull in a third person to disperse some of the strain of maintaining a relationship. This makes a triad or tri- angle. In the language of FST, a triangle can handle the tension inherent in any relationship easier than a dyad and may be help- ful or constructive. That's because the tension can be spread out among three people rather than two. In this situation each per- son's emotional load is lightened. If you've ever sat down with your best friend and vented about your co-parent, you've cre- ated a triangle.

While triangles pull more people into the relationship, they may also serve to push someone out. This can develop into one of the persons being the "odd man out," someone with a dimin- ished sense of power in the relationship. The triangle becomes problematic when this odd man out tries to regain a primary position and pushes someone else to the outside. Again, this isn't always a conscious effort, but rather a subtle, emotionally driven response to a shift in a relationship.

In Chad and Rachel's relationship, all kinds of triangles come into play. Some kind of mother/father/child triangle happens in nearly every new family. This is almost impossible to avoid sim- ply because children tend to bond with their mothers first.

In Chad and Rachel's case, their personal anxieties about their relationship are pulling baby Jason into the triangle. Rather than dealing with her frustrations by talking with Chad, Rachel is pouring her energy into Jason in an unconscious effort to diffuse the situation. Chad is also creating a triangle with Rachel and Jason every time he lets Rachel take over the parenting. He feels unsure about how to parent Jason, so he shifts the focus of his anxiety onto his relationship with Rachel.

Then there is the triangle of Chad, Rachel, and Rachel's mother. This is a common and potentially powerful triangle for new parents. When a woman becomes a mother, she often connects with her own mother in a new way. Even if they don't get along, the mother/adult daughter relationship shifts when the daughter becomes a mother. Now that Rachel is a mother, she finds that she wants to talk with her mom more often and frequently seeks her advice on how to care for Jason. The women create their own triangle, with Chad being the odd man. Rachel's mother has, in effect, become the third parent.

Even when the third person isn't physically present, she can be an integral part of a triangle. Chad's mother, Gloria, is a great example. Chad often gets frustrated with Rachel because he feels like her expectations of him are unreasonably high. Subconsciously, he would like her to be more like his mom. He wishes she would let him do things in his own time and in his own way. This creates a triangle as Chad pulls Gloria into his relationship with Rachel. Rachel is doing much the same thing. She finds herself thinking about how her mother functioned and managed their household when Rachel was a child. She often compares herself as a mother to her own mother. Mostly she feels like she falls short. As a result, she experiences tremendous anxiety, which she takes out on Chad.

Triangles can serve useful purposes in relationships. However, when they become problematic they allow couples to avoid real issues, since they diffuse the tension between the two people. But feeling like you've dealt with a problem and actually dealing with it are not the same thing. Triangles also exacerbate problems because they can create hurt feelings and a sense of alienation in the person who becomes the odd man or woman out. (For clarity, FST uses the terms the *insider* vs. the *outsider*.) Looking at these triangles in Chad and Rachel's relationship, it's not hard to see who the insiders and outsiders are in each triangle. The problems that create the triangles only get worse when the outsider starts pushing to regain an inside position. When one of the insiders teams up with the outsider, the former insider gets pushed out.

> **Genogram:** As you work on your genogram, look for triangles in your family. Listen for the ways family members talk *about* instead of *to* one another. You might hear your grandmother say that her mother-in-law was critical of her parenting. You may learn that Aunt Bessie was always getting into trouble, while Uncle Mike was a delightful child. Notice how family members consciously and unconsciously team up in times of stress. Try to figure out who are the outsiders and who are the insiders in the various triangles you observe.

Differentiation of Self

Triangles happen because of the ways we are affected by other people. We often think and act in response to the spoken and unspoken expectations of others. Chad's mother, for example, never told him outright that she would take care of all of his problems. Her actions and attitude toward him, however, sent that message loud and clear. For Chad it's quite natural, therefore, to assume that someone else will take care of him.

Rachel, of course, grew up with a different message. She was taught that she could always do more, do it better, and do it on her own. Her choices are a response to her feelings of inadequacy. Her fear of disappointing others is in tension with her expectation that she can and should do things herself.

Confronting this natural tendency to think and act in response to others is what FST refers to as *differentiation of self*.

Differentiation is our ability to understand ourselves as separate from other people, particularly those who are closest to us. Being poorly differentiated doesn't necessarily mean a person is always trying to please others or that a person can't think for himself. A low level of differentiation can actually come out as rebellion, which is essentially a negative response to other people and not a genuine expression of the self. A highly differentiated person tends to form her own opinions and make decisions and life choices based on her own instincts and ideas.

Differentiation is not the same as disconnection. Differentiation isn't about emotional closeness. Differentiation is about influence and control. Chad is actually more differentiated from his mother than you might expect, but he is certainly not disconnected from her. He doesn't worry about seeking her approval (he has always had it), and he feels the freedom to be himself with her. But he is poorly differentiated from his father. Growing up, Chad often acted out just to see if his dad would react. His shoplifting arrest is one such incident. Chad has made conscious decisions about his career and lifestyle in an effort to be different from his dad. This is an example of a person making choices in response to others, rather than from their own sense of self.

Rachel, then, is poorly differentiated from her mother. Clearly, she worries a great deal about what her mother will think of her and continues to order her life around her approval. This is true particularly in her new maternal role. That Rachel married a guy like Chad is evidence of her inability to differentiate. She was attracted to the parts of his personality that are precisely the opposite of her mother's personality. (She may not have been *consciously* seeking someone on the opposite end of the personality spectrum.) Her choice of husband was undoubtedly influenced by a deep-seated desire to live with a different kind of person.

Unfortunately, Chad and Rachel are not differentiated from each other. They have both made reactive choices rather than conscious proactive choices. Chad quickly gave up many of his efforts to connect with Jason because he doesn't want to deal with Rachel's criticisms. Rachel bought into Chad's willingness to let her take over. That made it possible for her to avoid her anxieties about his approach to parenting.

At the heart of the concept of differentiation is the idea of *fusion*. Fusion is the connection that exists between two people, and it can be positive or negative. Negative fusion means seeking control by trying to be *unlike* another person. Chad tells himself he doesn't want to be anything like his father. He makes life choices based on this need to be different. That's negative fusion. Chad is not making differentiated choices. Chad is still being controlled by his relationship with his father.

The term "positive fusion" sounds, well, positive. But it is actually just as destructive to relationships. Positive fusion is seeking control by acting in a way that will earn that person's acceptance. Rachel is positively fused to her mother. That is, she works very hard to make choices that will win her mother's approval.

Genogram: The point of understanding the concept of differentiation is not that we dismiss the influence of our families. Rather, the purpose is to recognize the ways our families impact us. The goal is to make healthy, *intentional* choices about what we want to carry with us as we form families of our own. The patterns of differentiation in a family are often clear. Nearly every family member makes at least a few choices unconsciously or with the intention of controlling the responses of other family members. But the people you interview for your genogram might not always admit this intent. They may not even be aware of it. So listen for phrases like: "She was just like her mother," or "He was always trying to get people to notice him." It's important to understand your own level of differentiation as you move into parenthood. That will make it possible for you and your co-parent to make intentional decisions for your family. Your choices will come from your beliefs, desires, and instincts rather than from a desire to illicit certain responses from others.

Emotional Cutoff

Emotional cutoff is exactly what it sounds like, radical separation. A cutoff is a person's effort to distance herself from a family or family member. A cutoff is usually an effort to control the level of tension by putting extreme limits on the relationship. It doesn't necessarily mean a complete end to contact of any kind. In Chad's case, he has created an emotional cutoff with his father. When Chad calls home, he rarely, if ever, talks to his dad. When Chad and Rachel visit Chad's family, Chad avoids conversation with his father. An emotional cutoff is an extreme form of fusion—the motivation for the cutoff is to get a response from the other person. At some level, Chad wants his father to react to the lack of contact between them, although this is an unconscious desire.

In an emotional cutoff, the person who does the cutting off typically forges a more intense relationship with a third party. This happens in an effort to meet his or her emotional needs. Chad's relationship with his mother is a good example. Part of his continued fusion with Gloria is the result of the cutoff with his father. Chad's relationship with Rachel has also been affected by the emotional cutoff with his father. When they first began dating, Chad was deeply attracted to Rachel. He fell in love with her quickly. The intensity of his feelings for her was exaggerated by the emotional cutoff with his father. Chad is in danger of putting all of his emotional eggs in Rachel's basket because he needs her so much.

Chad is also prone to using his son as both a weapon and a shield in his relationship with his father. After Jason's birth, Chad's parents came to see the new baby. During this visit Chad and his father spoke very little. However, Chad spent a great deal of time bonding with his mother. He talked to her about fatherhood and listened to her stories about his own infancy. Jason became a way for Chad to deepen the gap between his father and himself. Jason also became a pathway to an even more firm attachment to his mother. Chad's cutoff with his father demonstrates Chad's fear that he might be like his father

after all. Chad's failure to bond quickly with his son only confirms these fears. Because of the cutoff, Chad has an even
greater need to attach to his son than might be expected.

Emotional cutoffs are not always obvious. Some emotional
cutoffs take the form of a family member moving far away and
not visiting home very often. There might never be an obvious
disconnection, but rather a gradual slipping away of the relationship. They can also pop up when something in the family
system changes. A person may be able to tolerate a difficult
relationship with her family of origin under ordinary circumstances. When she has a child, however, she may find that she
doesn't want to expose her kids to the family's perceived dys-
functionality. She might therefore create an emotional cutoff
from the rest of the family when a baby enters the picture.

Genogram: You may have a hard time finding the emotional cutoffs
that might exist in your family system because they are often subtle or
camouflaged. This is an area where you'll need to listen to what *isn't*
said as much as to what *is* said. If there is an uncle no one talks about
much, check out the reasons why. Maybe a sibling has moved far away
and rarely returns home. What reasons do the sibling and other family
members give? If some people in the family stopped speaking to each
other for a time, find out why. Then look for connections between the
emotional cutoffs and the levels of differentiation. Talk with your co-
parent about any emotional cutoffs in your immediate family. How
have these impacted you and the rest of your family?

Multigenerational Transmission Process

The concept of the multigenerational transmission process
(MTP) describes how small differences in the levels of differentiation between parents and their children change the family
with each generation. The concept of MTP suggests that the
roots of current behavior run generations deep.

For Chad and Rachel to make headway in their relationship, they need to begin to understand the ways in which they—and their families—have been formed over time. It would be helpful for each of them to spend some time speaking with their parents. They need to gain a better understanding of the assumptions their own mothers and fathers brought into the family. These are the assumptions that played a part in shaping Chad and Rachel's childhood. Chad and Rachel must learn to recognize them and make conscious choices about the patterns they want to repeat and those they want to break. They have to figure out how to differentiate themselves from their families.

Rachel and Chad will also need to pay attention to the ways in which their relationship with Jason reflects their levels of differentiation. Chad may find himself having unreasonable expectations about his relationship with Jason. Chad wants a relationship with Jason that is unlike his relationship with his own father, and he has high hopes that he and Jason will be best buddies. He wants to believe he will always be there for his son in all the ways his father wasn't there for him. Because his relationship with his dad was lacking, he idealizes the potential father-son relationship with Jason. So his expectations of himself have been shaped largely in reaction to his father rather than by his own vision of what it means to be a good parent.

Rachel will need to understand her family legacy as well. She will need to recognize her tendency to have high expectations of her son, particularly as he gets older. Because her mother expected so much from her, Rachel's natural instinct will be to withhold affection and acceptance unless Jason meets her expectations.

Genogram: After you have interviewed at least two generations of your family, look for the ways differentiation has changed from one generation to the next. Explore ways individuals have shifted the level of differentiation. How do you and your siblings compare? How is differentiation playing out in your siblings' families?

Family Projection Process

The family projection process happens when parents pass their emotional issues on to their children. Children then begin to react to the problems their parents perceive in them, thereby confirming the perception that there is a problem. Chad's mother, for example, often worried that her husband didn't spend enough time with the children. She tried to compensate by spending more time with them. Eventually, the children learned to turn to their mother to meet their emotional needs. This, in turn, further distanced them from their father. Chad's mother projected her anxiety onto her children. In the process she helped create precisely the problem she was hoping to solve.

Family projection follows a three-step process. First, the parents over-focus on a child out of fear that something is wrong with the child. Second, the child responds to the parents' anxiety by acting out—increased tantrums or worry, for instance— which confirms the parents' fears. Finally, the parents treat the child as if something is really wrong. Basically, the parents' fears create an environment in which the child develops the behavior the parents were concerned about in the first place.

The death of Rachel's father obviously created a number of issues in Rachel's family, including an interesting example of the projection process. Rachel's mother was afraid she was not strong enough to take care of the children by herself. She didn't want the children to worry about her or pick up on her fears about being a single parent, so she didn't cry or grieve her husband's death in front of her children. Given their own uncertainty about how to deal with their grief, their mother's apparent lack of crying made the children feel less secure. Rachel and her siblings were unsure of how to respond to their father's death because they had no model of appropriate grief. They worried that their own emotions might be wrong or abnormal. Rachel's mother therefore planted the seeds of the very insecurity from which she was trying to save them.

Projection comes out of the fear all parents have that something bad will happen to their kids. Chad's mother had a tendency to step in and solve her son's problems. This behavior was based on her belief that he couldn't handle difficult situations by himself. As a result, he has trouble doing just that. It is also true, however, that the projection process can sometimes create a problem opposite to the one the parent feared. For example, as Jason gets older, Rachel will have to find ways to deal with her concerns about being a working mother. She will have to avoid projecting that Jason won't be close to her as a result of her working. Rachel will have to resist the temptation to smother him with love and attention to compensate for the time they are apart. She will have to work hard to let Jason develop a healthy level of independence even when she wants him to need her.

> **Genogram:** Ask both parents and children about family fears and anxieties. Find out what worries children might have sensed in their parents. Contrast this with what the parents actually worried about. Look for the places where a projection became reality. How did that impact the family? What issues were projected onto you? How did you respond to the projections of your parents?

Societal Emotional Process

The same issues that show up in the family system are also present in the way society functions. When there are stressors in a society—say an increase in violent crime—the society will work to find ways to alleviate that stress. Consider the way the court system often echoes the parent-child relationship, and you can see how this plays out. The essential lesson here is that FST is never far away from us. We live in it whether we're at home or simply living our lives in the context of a broader culture. The idea that these concepts are carried out in society may seem unrelated to your life as a new parent, but it's worth thinking about the systems in which you and your child will function. That includes the church, the school system, and even the legal system.

Chad and Rachel both grew up in the church, but they have not been members of a church since college. They attend a church in their neighborhood when they feel like it. So far, they have not made any kind of commitment to that church. With Jason's arrival, they both felt it was important to take faith formation more seriously. Chad likes the church in their neighborhood. There are several couples their age, and the pastor seems nice enough. Rachel, however, isn't sure. There aren't many young children in the congregation for Jason to play with, and she is concerned that Jason would have trouble finding friends there as he got older. She also doesn't like attending church on Sunday mornings, since that schedule interferes with Jason's morning nap, leaving him grumpy for the rest of the day. Rachel hoped they could find a church that met in the evening. Chad didn't like the idea of giving up one of their weekend nights to church.

In this case, Chad and Rachel are butting up against what is essentially another family system. They not only have to come to terms with their individual experiences and expectations of church, they have to make their way through the "family history" of the church institution itself. They can do that more easily if they recognize the ways in which a church system is very much like a family system, complete with triangles, varying levels of differentiation, and deeply entrenched "rules." While they may not be able to do anything about the church family system, simply seeing the church in this way can help them readjust their expectations and requirements in their search for the best church home.

Genogram: Ask questions about social issues, particularly those experienced by previous generations of your family. If your grandparents grew up during the Depression, explore the ways in which that experience impacted them. What other societal issues played a part in your family story?

The concepts involved in FST can seem unwieldy at first. So don't worry about mastering everything in the first week. Each session will take you through a more in-depth discussion of these concepts and show you how they apply to your family life. As you begin to see them at work in your family, you will be able to develop a fuller understanding of how you have been impacted by your family system. More importantly, you will have the tools you need to develop your own family system, one that helps you create the best family life possible for you and your child.

Appendix B

Creating a Genogram

Families take many forms these days. No longer can we assume that a person grew up as the biological child of two parents who have only ever been married to one another. Instead, families come in all shapes and sizes—though they're generally smaller today than a generation ago—and with so many various combinations of relationships, it is hard to generalize about "the family." But one thing every family has is a family tree.

When people hear the phrase "family tree," they may think of genealogy and family history, dusty attics filled with long forgotten relics, or a heavy, old, oversized leather Bible with unfamiliar names written in it. In *Shaping Your Family's Future*, family trees include genealogical information like that, and much more, because the focus is on the relationships within your family, past and present. To help you become the best parent you can be, we want to guide you through an investigation of the patterns of relationships evident within your generation and across the generations. To uncover the richness of our families of origin and their importance for how we will parent our own children, we must look closely at several aspects of life within our families. The tool we use for achieving this goal is to complete a genogram.

In brief, a genogram is a diagram of all the people in your extended family, and in that regard it is much like a family tree. What makes it different from a traditional genealogy, or family tree, are the information and observations you add about their patterns of relationship. On top of that, your genogram is a valuable tool for giving you insights into how your family functions, and based on these insights you can choose which traditions to embrace and pass on to your children and which not to perpetuate. Fortunately, the hard work of becoming a parent is much easier when you can step back and take a close look at the factors that shaped you as a person and influenced your notions of the kind of parent you want (or ought) to be for your children.

Many things about our family are beyond our control. For instance, we don't get to choose our parents or siblings, or our grandparents, aunts, uncles, and cousins. Nor do we choose whether our parents stay together or get divorced, or the stepparent and stepbrothers and stepsisters that might be added to our family after a divorce.

✚ What is a Genogram? ✚

A genogram is like a family tree, but with a focus on relationships. Your genogram will begin as a blank sheet of paper or blank electronic file. By the time you complete your genogram, however, it will be filled with the unique combination of squares and circles, lines and symbols, names and information, that represent your family.

A typical family tree shows each individual in the family, and information about those individuals, such as their gender, and dates of birth, marriage, and death. In addition, it sketches the basic connections between these individuals: grandparents, parents, siblings, aunts and uncles, grandchildren. What makes a genogram different from a family tree or genealogy are the added texture and details about the individuals and their family relationships. Along with naming family members and filling in as much basic information about them as you have available (i.e., the kind of data you would find on a census form), your genogram includes observations about emotional connections, methods of communication, family traditions, roles, rules, and boundaries. Through this combination of personal descriptions and relational observations, the genogram reveals patterns of relationships in your family, which you might not notice if you would never gather all the information and record it in one place. Once you can see these patterns, you can determine which patterns you want to embrace, which you want to modify, and which you want to discard, as you shape the future of your own family. If you want to take the genogram a step further, you can build what is called an ecomap, using the genogram as a foundation. Ecomaps are a way to set your genogram in context. They provide more detailed depictions of the social forces that impact individuals and their family system, which can help you understand events, actions, and why things happened in your family at a given time and place.

The genogram is a tool to help you become a whole human being, both on your own and in relation to your family; the two are inseparable. It is more than a series of exercises through which you produce a chart with boxes and circles. While the genogram itself is a mere graphic representation of personal and familial information, in reality it is a touchstone from which you can explore your family and yourself. As you think about the key elements that shape you individually, as you consider what kind of parent you want to be, and family legacy you wish to pass on to your child or children, the process of creating your genogram equips you to identify and evaluate key factors from your past, so you can determine how best to experience individual wellness and relational healing and wholeness.

You can create your family's genogram through a combination of several resources and activities. Some of these resources are readily available on the Internet or your local public library. You can find other print and electronic resources through family genealogy organizations and even stored in the attic of your grandparents' house. But the most valuable resources are your living relatives. If you truly want to create a tool that will help you understand how your family relates to one another, there is no better place to start than with the people most directly involved in shaping the family—your mom and dad, brothers and sisters, grandparents, aunts and uncles, cousins, great aunts and uncles, second cousins, as far and wide as you have the time, stamina, and resources to pursue the details of your family's relational traditions.

✛ The Parts of a Genogram ✛

Shaping Your Family's Future introduces you to the basic concepts of family systems theory. A genogram uses the concepts of Family Systems Theory (FST) to make sense of various types of information that you will gather from the resources available to you. The genogram you'll be doing for this course is a shorter version of a project that can take months, or even years. If you want to take a crack at a more detailed family history, the book *Genograms: Assessment and Intervention*, by Monica McGoldrick, Randy Gerson, and Sylvia Shellenberger, is a terrific resource. You can find information on this and other resources at the end of this Appendix and at the end of each chapter.

In the simplified six-step genogram presented here in *Shaping Your Family's Future*, you begin with a basic blank genogram chart and return again and again to this chart, adding more and more layers of detail with each return visit. First, you supply personal information about the individuals in your immediate and extended family. Next, you diagram the relationships between these individuals. Then you gather details about how your family as a whole and individually relate, communicate, and are made up emotionally. After that, using symbols, abbreviations, and words, you illustrate family relationships and your own role in the family. Based on what you learn from the genogram process, you write out a description of yourself, your role in the family, how the family functions, and the family traditions. Finally, you can decide what kind of person you want to be, what kind of co-parent you want to be, what kind of parent you want to be, how you wish to relate to your family, what you want to do with its traditions, and how you want to shape your own family's future by who you are and how you go about parenting your child(ren).

The Genogram Chart

As a graphic representation of your family's relationships, a genogram consists of squares and circles labeled with personal information, as well as lines and symbols representing how these individuals are related and how they relate to one another on various levels. This section will explain the symbols and their meanings.

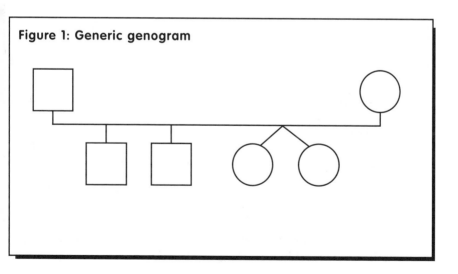

Figure 1: Generic genogram

1. Genogram symbols

1. Gender symbols
2. Children and birth symbols

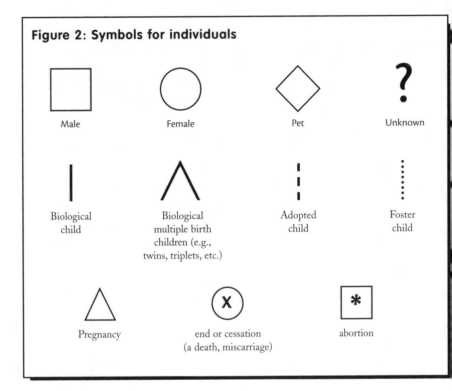

Figure 2: Symbols for individuals

Male	Female	Pet	Unknown
Biological child	Biological multiple birth children (e.g., twins, triplets, etc.)	Adopted child	Foster child
Pregnancy	end or cessation (a death, miscarriage)	abortion	

3. Interpersonal relationship symbols

The types of interpersonal relationships between two individuals are indicated with symbols as described below. Each relationship is indicated with a short vertical line below the two parties. So, for example, if a man and woman are married, you represent this with a square on the left with a short solid line descending, and a circle in the right with a short solid line descending, and a solid horizontal line connecting the two short vertical lines.

Figure 3: Interpersonal relationships symbols

▬▬▬▬▬▬

Solid horizontal line = marriage (religious, civil union), or familial connection (e.g., siblings)

━ ━ ━ ━ ━

Horizontal line of long dashes (em dash) separated by spaces = engagement

▬▬▬▬▬▬▬

Horizontal line of medium-sized dashes (en dash) separated by spaces = engagement and cohabitation

---

▬ ▬ ▬ ▬ ▬ ▬ ▬

Horizontal line of short dashes (hyphens) followed by spaces = legal cohabitation

▬ ▬ ● ▬ ▬ ● ▬ ▬

Horizontal line of two short dashes (hyphens) followed by a single dot = committed nonlegalized cohabitation

▬ ▬ ●●●● ▬ ▬ ●●●● ▬ ▬

Horizontal line of two short dashes (hyphens) followed by four dots = uncommitted nonlegalized cohabitation

---

●●●●●●●●●●●●●●●●●●●●●

Series of horizontal dots = Dating

▬ ● ▬ ● ▬ ● ▬ ● ▬

Series of dashes and dots separated by spaces = Temporary relationship or one-night stand

✳ ✳ ✳ ✳ ✳ ✳ ✳ ✳

Series of asterisks separated by spaces = rape or forced relationship

---

4. Relationship dynamics symbols
Describing the formal relationship between two people is one thing. Capturing the dynamics of that relationship are a different sort of thing. Relationships are ever-changing and dynamic, which means that what applies at one moment may not later on. Use these symbols to indicate changes in the dynamics of the relationships described in your genogram.

Figure 4: Symbols for relationships

Single back slash on any of the relationship symbols = separation in fact (living apart, or emotional separation)

Single forward slash on any of the relationship symbols = legal separation

Double forward slash on any of the relationship symbols = complete break (divorce)

Triple forward slash on any of the relationship symbols = annulment

X on any of the relationship symbols = death in the relationhip (widow, widower, death of live-in partner)

5. Emotional relationship symbols

The types of emotional relationships between two individuals are indicated with symbols as described below. In contrast to interpersonal relationships, the symbols for emotional relationships connect the two people directly, not involving the short vertical line below the two parties. So, using the example of a man and woman who are married, the square and circle will each have a short solid line below it, and these short vertical lines will be connected with a solid horizontal line. However, if the husband and wife fight all the time and have a pretty volatile relationship, that emotional relationship would be represented by a wavy line directly between the square and circle.

Figure 5: Symbols for emotional relationships

----- || -----

Cutoff /estranged relationship = medium dashes with two vertical lines in the middle

· · · · · · · · · · · · · · · · · · · ·

Indifferent / apathetic relationship = dots

-- -- -- -- -- -- -- --

Distant / poor relationship = medium dashes

-- -- -- -- -- -- -- -- --

Close / friendship relationship = two parallel lines of dashes

———————

Plain normal relationship = single straight solid line

═══════════

Intimate relationship = two parallel straight solid lines

═══════════

Fused relationship = three parallel straight solids lines

Hostile / conflictual relationship = single solid wavy line

Distant-hostile relationship = single solid wavy line over medium dashed line

Close-hostile relationship = single solid wavy line over two parallel straight solid lines

Fused-hostile relationship = single solid wavy line over three parallel straight solid lines

Violent relationship = single solid jagged squiggly line

Distant violent relationship = single solid jagged squiggly line over medium dashed line

Close violent relationship = single solid jagged squiggly line over two parallel straight solid lines

Fused violent relationship = single solid jagged squiggly line over three parallel straight solid lines

Abuse (unknown type) = single solid mountain peak-type line over a single solid jagged squiggly line

Physical abuse = single solid mountain peak-type line

Sexual abuse = double solid tight jagged line

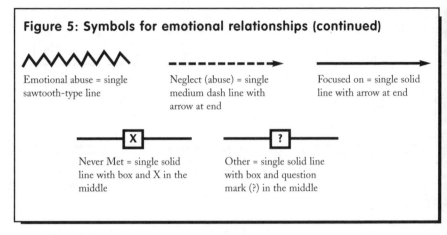

Figure 5: Symbols for emotional relationships (continued)

Emotional abuse = single sawtooth-type line

Neglect (abuse) = single medium dash line with arrow at end

Focused on = single solid line with arrow at end

Never Met = single solid line with box and X in the middle

Other = single solid line with box and question mark (?) in the middle

6. Mode of communication symbols

Since communication is such a complex activity, with a huge number of possible ways to do it depending on all the variables involved, it would be very hard to boil the variables down into a few simple symbols. To express patterns of communication in the genogram, draw a line between the two people and use the following symbols:

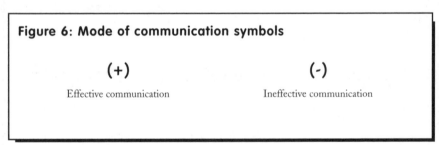

Figure 6: Mode of communication symbols

(+)

Effective communication

(-)

Ineffective communication

7. Faith symbols

However we decide to practice our religion, our family traditions and our personal choice overlap. On the genogram, the more accurately you can show both the family traditions and how each individual practices his or her religion, the more clearly you will see how your own religious commitments relate to your family and the individuals in it. From the following list, choose the symbol that represents the religious tradition of both the family tradition and the individual. Also, indicate the frequency and degree of the individual's religious commitment. So, a devout Baptist Christian would be ✞(Baptist)-1, and a lapsed Jew would be ✡-4.

Figure 7: Faith symbols

✞   Christianity = a cross

     Catholic: Roman Catholic, Anglican, Episcopalian, Orthodox
     Protestant: Baptists, Brethren, Christian Church, Church of Christ, Church of God,
                Church of the Nazarene, Congregationalists, Disciples of Christ
                Lutherans, Evangelical Free Church, Methodists, Moravians,
                Pentecostals, Puritans, Quakers, Presbyterians, Reformed Church
     Other: Adventists, Church of Scientology, Jehovah's Witnesses, Moonies,
                Mormons, Salvation Army

✡   Judaism = a star of David   ☪   Islam = crescent and star

(H)   Hinduism = H in a circle   (B)   Buddhism = B in a circle

(C)   Confucianism = C in a circle   (☯)   Taoism = yin-yang symbol

⛩   Shintoism = torii gate   (TR)   Traditional religion = TR in a circle

(other)   Other religion = name the religion (At)   Atheist = At in a circle
       and circle it

                              ?   (?) = uncertain or unknown
(Ag)   Agnostic = Ag in a circle

1   Devout, frequent practice = 1   **2**   Moderate involvement, regular
                                practice = 2

3   Occasional involvement, infrequent **4**   Lapsed, non-practicing, nominal
     practice = 3   only = 4

2. Individual data

Name: full name including middle name and married
name, if different from name prior to marriage
Birth date
Marriage date
Separation or divorce date
Death date

3. Relational information and representation

Relational information depicts the family connections between the individuals listed on your genogram. The primary relationships are between co-parents (spouses), parents and children, and between siblings. All nuclear relationships consist of at least two people.

Beyond the one-on-one relationships, the next broader relational unit is the nuclear family. Every nuclear family unit consists of two co-parents and at least one child. Even where a single parent currently lives with the child, two parents produced that child, and so both parents should be represented in the genogram.

Parental, sibling, aunt, uncle, cousin, and other familial relationships are indicated by the connection of symbols described. If there is no relationship, the two individuals should not be connected by any lines or symbols.

4. Emotional information and representation

Adding symbols to indicate the types of emotional connections between individuals gives the genogram a level of depth missing in traditional family trees. You can only accurately represent the emotional relationships after doing your research, speaking with family members, and reflecting on your own memories. While you may remember a warm and lovable grandma, you may get another picture altogether from your mother or father, which may give you a more balanced picture of your grandma. Therefore, the emotional relationship between any given individual and any one person can either be the same as, or differ from, that individual's emotional relationship with any other persons in the family genogram. If your genogram gets overly busy and confusing because of all the symbols and lines, you may need to create copies of the simplified version without any indicators of emotional relationship before adding those emotional symbols for each family unit.

5. Communication information and representation

In every relationship, the people involved establish patterns of communication that combine many factors. These include such elements as the relational pattern of each person, ways the family used to communicate, the circumstances surrounding and topic of conversation, the mental and physical health of the persons involved, and all other factors that make up the life situation of the individuals who are communicating with one another. Identifying how people communicate can illuminate how the family relates emotionally, as well as other patterns and traditions within the family.

People communicate in lots of different ways. Mostly we use verbal, written or graphic, and nonverbal forms of communication, and we communicate on both conscious and subconscious levels. When we attempt to communicate we begin with certain assumptions about how the world operates, we think of a message and choose a means of expressing the message, we communicate within a specific context, we target a specific recipient or recipients for the message, and we expect the person who receives our message to decode the message. Individuals communicate, as do entire families, in manifold ways, on multiple levels, and in various contexts. It should come as no surprise that the lack or failure of communication is a major contributor to problems in family relationships.

✜ Genogram Homework ✜

The homework assigned for each session is designed to be a series of genogram building blocks. You start with the basics of identifying family members, providing personal information about each one, and diagramming their family connections. Then comes the more time-consuming and rewarding work of talking with family members about specific relational issues raised in *Shaping Your Family's Future*. These encounters are supposed to shed light on your faith, your self, your relationship with your co-parent, your parenting preferences, your family, and your community. Some of the conversations you have may feel uncomfortable; others may bring great joy and be life changing and freeing. Make them as rewarding as possible without feeling like you have to ask all the proposed questions, get all the details, or talk to every person in your family. Just spending time with members of your family can be valuable in itself.

Each chapter of *Shaping Your Family's Future* will provide a list of questions that relate to that chapter's theme. These questions aren't meant to be a definitive list—feel free to use as many as you like, and to add your own as well. Really, the questions you ask are less important than the answers you get. As you talk to other members of your family, listen for the emotions behind the stories. Listen to what they *don't* say as well as what they *do* say. Look for patterns in relationships. Try to spot connections in family attitudes. This book offers some ideas on how to interpret the stories you hear.

✜ Samples of each step of the genogram ✜

Figures 8 to 13 describe the six steps in creating a genogram.

Figure 8: Genogram Step 1: Basic family unit

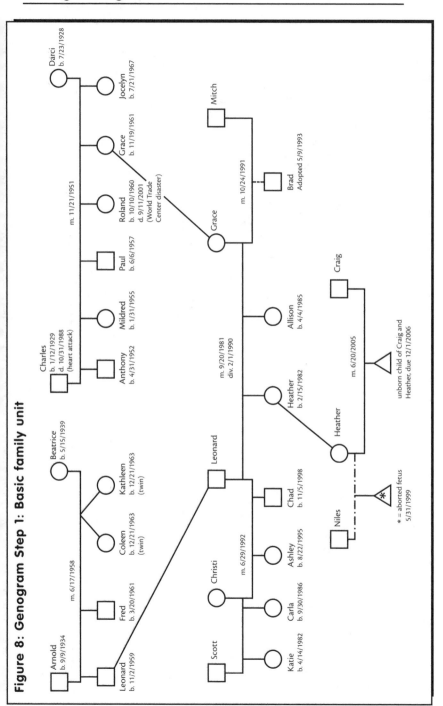

Figure 9: Genogram Step 2: Faith traditions of the family

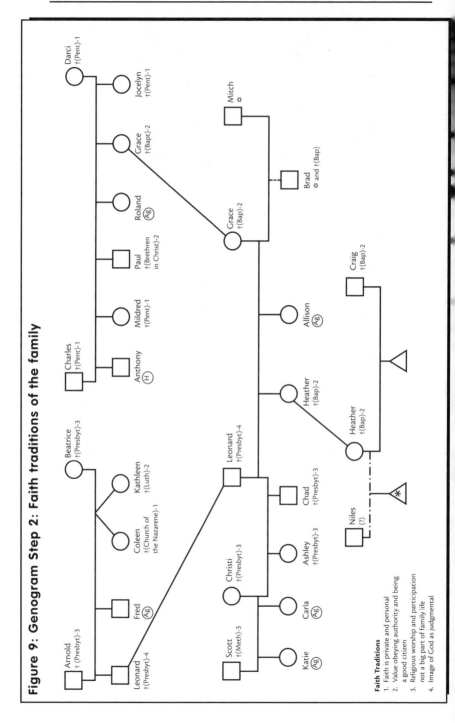

Faith Traditions

1. Faith is private and personal
2. Value obeying authority and being a good citizen
3. Religious worship and participation not a big part of family life
4. Image of God as judgmental

Figure 10: Genogram Step 3: Individual personality and family roles and rules

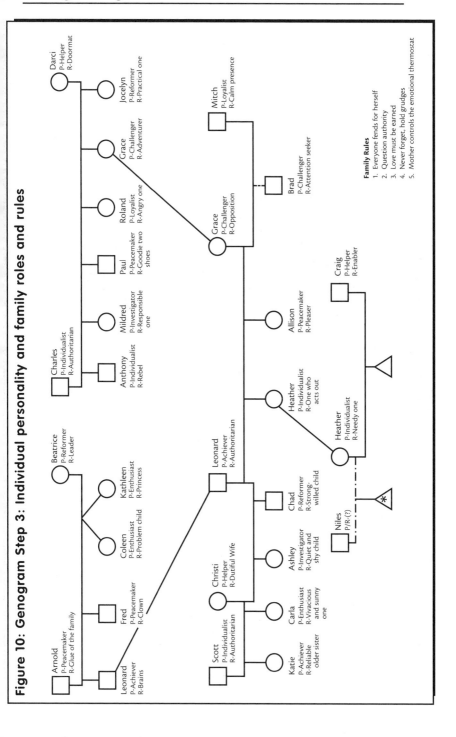

Family Rules
1. Everyone fends for herself
2. Question authority
3. Love must be earned
4. Never forget, hold grudges
5. Mother controls the emotional thermostat

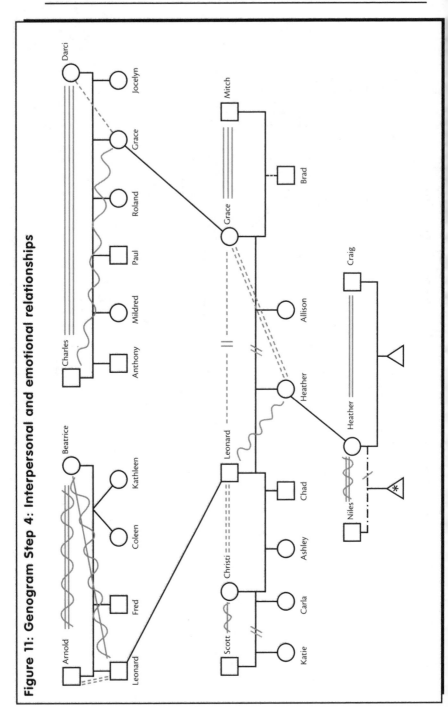

Figure 11: Genogram Step 4: Interpersonal and emotional relationships

Figure 12: Genogram Step 5: Parenting, communication, and conflict

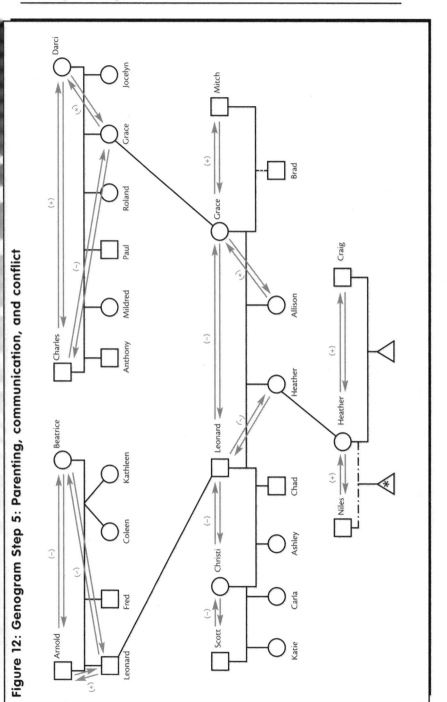

Figure 13: Genogram Step 6: Family and community

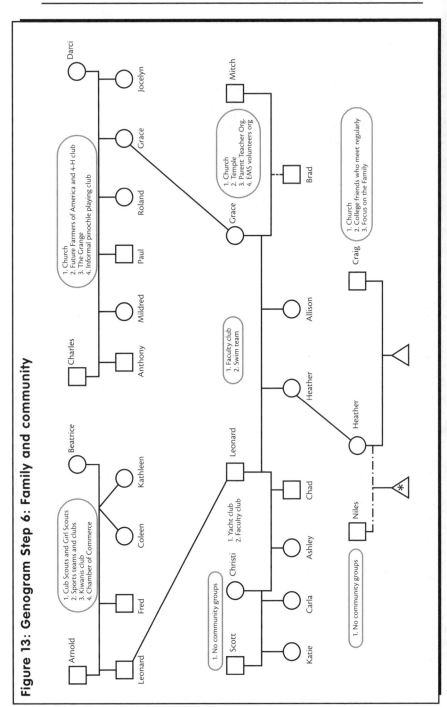

✚ Genogram Resource ✚

McGoldrick, Monica, Randy Gerson, and Sylvia Shellenberger. *Genograms: Assessment and Intervention.* New York: W. W. Norton, 1999.

✠ Notes ✠

✠ Notes ✠

✚ Notes ✚

✠ Notes ✠

✛ Notes ✛

_____

_____

_____

_____

_____

_____

_____

_____

_____

_____

_____

_____

_____

_____

_____

_____

_____

_____

_____

✠ Notes ✠

✠ Notes ✠

✛ Notes ✛

✚ Notes ✚